A Line of Power

A Line of Power

Andrew Strathern

Tavistock Publications   *London and New York*

'There is a line of power which stretches
from Port Moresby to here,
but we have not found it yet.'

Ongka

First published in 1984 by
Tavistock Publications
11 New Fetter Lane,
London EC4P 4EE

Published in the USA by
Tavistock Publications
in association with Methuen, Inc.
733 Third Avenue, New York
NY 10017

© 1984 Andrew Strathern

Typeset by
Scarborough Typesetting Services
and printed in Great Britain
at the University Press, Cambridge

British Library Cataloguing in
Publication Data

Strathern, Andrew
A line of power. –
(Social science paperbacks; no. 268)
1. Highlands (Papua New Guinea
– Social conditions
I. Title   II. Series
303.4'0995'5   HN932.H5

ISBN 0–422–78890–2
ISBN 0–422–78900–3 Pbk

Library of Congress Cataloging in
Publication Data

Strathern, Andrew.
A line of power.
Bibliography: p.
Includes indexes.
1. Melpa (Papua New Guinea
people)   2. Pangia (Papua New
Guinea people)   3. Social change –
Case studies.
I. Title.
IU740.42.S77   1984
306'.0899912   84–2521

ISBN 0–422–78890–2
ISBN 0–422–78900–3 (pbk.)

Contents

Acknowledgements

I am most grateful to the Administration and later the Independent Government of Papua New Guinea and to authorities in the Western and Southern Highlands Provinces for permitting me to live there on many occasions since 1964 in order to do fieldwork. I am grateful also the numerous bodies which have supported the research financially: the University of Cambridge, the Australian National University, the University of Papua New Guinea, University College, London, and the Institute of Papua New Guinea Studies, Port Moresby. Specific field funds were also granted during 1977–82 by the British Social Science Research Council. Academic colleagues and personal companions have taught me a great deal in all of the places and institutions in which I have worked, and foremost among these is Marilyn Strathern, with whose ideas mine have been intertwined, as the Melpa say, like *op kan* and *pat kan*, the vines of yams and of winged beans: not always in agreement, but growing together. I owe, also, perhaps rather more than most anthropologists to the very close relationships which I have maintained with friends among the Hagen and Pangia people during the last twenty years. Finally, my thanks to Mrs Kathy Kituai and especially to Ms Mitasila Simati for typing the manuscript.

Andrew Strathern

Institute of Papua New Guinea Studies
Port Moresby, 1984

1 Introduction

Anthropologists working in the Highlands Provinces of Papua New Guinea have been faced with two somewhat contradictory tasks: first, to understand these Highlands societies as forms in themselves; and second, to analyse the numerous recent changes that have occurred in the lives of the Highlanders. In principle these two tasks are separate; in practice they have proved hard to disentangle, for the simple reason that we rarely have adequate information stretching back over time and our observations have always been made in a context of induced changes. There is, therefore, no simple empirical solution to the question of change. Theoretical ideas must be brought into the discussion. Yet no unified overall approach has so far been developed to examine social change, either in general or in the ethnographic region with which I am here concerned. Nor is it my intention to develop or test any such approach through this book. I do, however, attempt to evaluate the main explanations adduced so far for the patterns of rapid change observed in the Highlands and to put forward a combination of cultural and sociological analysis as the best means of effectively penetrating certain apparent paradoxes in these patterns. The combination depends, in turn, on a re-statement of the old distinction between culture and society, and I must therefore begin with this distinction.

Essentially I argue that we have to comprehend the articulation of culture with social process, and it is on this articulation that the trajectory of change in a society depends. The cultural dimension in change has been either taken for granted or simply ignored in certain analyses of social change. Whereas anthropologists working in the synchronic mode have nearly always woven 'culture' firmly into their accounts, when they have turned to the topic of 'social change' they have felt obliged to employ only universalist sociological categories. In Melanesia, the confrontation between such 'emic' and 'etic' approaches emerged most clearly in the puzzled efforts of observers to explain new cult movements of a 'cargo' kind, since in these movements cultural elements were striking and impossible to ignore. But these elements are equally involved in all aspects of change, and must be given careful attention. In theoretical terms, such a focus on the inter-relations between cultural and social facts does not have any obvious intellectual forebears to fall back upon; but one way of formulating it is to say that ideally it would attempt the impossible task of uniting the perspectives of Weber and Marx. Another way of putting this is to say that the opposition between materialist and idealist or mentalist ways of explaining society is false, since ideas are in a sense 'material', and material objects are not significant unless they enter into social relations which are themselves defined by certain ideas. If there is, therefore, always an interplay of material and mental factors, then it is precisely that mediated interplay on which we would concentrate.

Before moving to the substantive discussion, however, I must explain what I mean by this contrast between cultural and sociological analysis, referring back to Gregory Bateson's consideration of the different points of view from which the ethnography of the Iatmul people could be presented (Bateson 1936). Bateson was interested in what he called ethos, eidos, and sociology. The first two belong to 'culture' and refer respectively to the tone and feeling of life as it is experienced and expressed by the actors, and to the structural form or forms to which life can be reduced through analysis. Sociology, in Bateson's usage, has to do with the functions of practices in terms of promoting or inhibiting the integration of social groups – an almost Radcliffe-Brownian definition. These distinctions are useful here, with the proviso that 'sociology' is defined more broadly as the study of social causes and effects, whether these are perceived by the actors and form a part of their own discourse or not. 'Culture', by contrast, is located firmly within the people's own discourse, again with the proviso that they may not consciously state the assumptions in terms of which they nevertheless act.

In neo-Marxist analysis, the main problem has been what to do with the classical Marxist metaphor or dogma of the relationship between base and superstructure. In this debate some have plumped for weakening the basic proposition so as to allow for 'degrees of freedom' between material determinants and cultural manifestations – Althusser has been influential in this regard. Others have reformulated it in terms of functions: religion, rather than other institutions may be dominant, but only if it also functions as a form of relation of production. Determination is still, therefore, referable to the base via the relations of production; this is essentially Maurice Godelier's solution. It presumes the idea of determination while allowing for the dominance in a given formation of any superstructural feature. While more definite than Althusser's position, this is perhaps open to suspicions of circularity in its argument. For if an institution is 'dominant', this surely means that it penetrates, or is involved in, all aspects of life, and therefore it will certainly function, *inter alia*, as a relation of production. This in itself does not tell us enough about determination. Such questions are intractable when seen only in synchronic terms, and must instead be handled historically (see Althusser 1969; Godelier 1978; Thompson 1978; Bloch 1983: 150–72).

It is important to remember in discussions of this kind that Marx's own chief interest lay in the workings of capital and capitalism in nineteenth century Europe. Neo-Marxist anthropologists have attempted to adapt Marx's ideas to the study of pre-capitalist societies, and in so doing have run into difficulties on two fronts: first, with regard to the interpretation of Marx's own theory, and second with the theory's applicability to the societies sudied by earlier anthropologists. Was Marx a techno-economic determinist? Most recent commentators have decided that he was not, but there is still the problem of what to do with the idea of the primacy of productive forces as against the relations of production. The productive forces consist of work and the instruments used to do the work of production. Measurement of their development is made by reference to the concept of surplus, but the rate of production of surplus in a given society is not simply a result of the productivity of labour, it rather results from production relations as a whole, so that in a sense it is impossible effectively to separate analytically the results of the productive forces alone on production. This leaves us once more with a composite notion of the social relations of production as the supposedly determining element of a given formation. The application of this concept to pre-capitalist societies is then made via the idea of exploitation. Relations of production are to be seen as relations of exploitation, by analogy with the workings of capitalism. Alex Callinicos, whose discussion of the problem I have followed here, quotes Marx: 'The specific economic form, in which unpaid surplus labour is pumped out of the direct producers, determines the relationship between rulers and ruled, as it grows out of production itself and, in turn, reacts upon it as a determining element.' But if there is an economic form, it is simultaneously a social form. Callinicos concludes on this topic that the level of the development of productive forces 'cannot be determined independently of social relations', but 'it nevertheless acts as a constraint upon or stimulus to changes in the relations of production'. This formulation does not exclude the possibility that other such stimuli or constraints also exist. He also adds: 'The relation of correspondence between forces and relations of production does not involve the causal primacy of either term but rather their mutual presupposition' (Callinicos 1982: 142 – 47).

The rest of Callinicos's discussion is concerned with the analysis of class struggle and a refutation of the idea that political power as such is determinant and not relationship to the means of production (here, then, he is defending classical Marxism). For pre-capitalist societies we are left with the question of what are the 'specific economic forms' by means of which unpaid surplus labour is activated. Presumably these economic forms should correspond to particular modes of production. But at the outset we have to decide whether the concept of 'unpaid labour' is applicable to the cases we wish to examine. In the case of capitalism its use is acceptable because a proportion of labour is paid for. But what of those cases where it is not a practice for anyone's labour to be directly paid for? Are we to seek for hidden forms of payment and therefore non-payment, or are we simply to use the idea as a metaphor expressing the relations of domination? What we have to look for is the equivalent of Marx's 'pumping mechanism'. In Hagen society this mechanism is quite definitely to be found in the *moka* exchange system. Both sexes work harder than they might otherwise do because they wish to participate in the *moka*. We would then conclude, within the terms of our present analytical vocabulary, that the *moka* functions as a relation of production. This is true, but it still leaves us with the question of ideology. What is the *moka*? It is an institution of exchange, built on ideas of reciprocity in persons and things and the prestige to be derived from successful pursuit of competitive giving and receiving – again, in a way which is very different from market-place trade but which may be seen as the analogue of such trade in its role as 'fetish', i.e. the 'fantastic form' in which the relations of production appear. At this point in the exposition, I have the feeling that the Marxist terms can be translated quite satisfactorily into ordinary language: 'Men and women work hard to raise pigs for the *moka*. They give these pigs away and expect to get greater returns later. In so far as men gain the greater prestige, there is an element of exploitation of women in the system, but women do have claims on the pigs they rear and no man would entirely ignore these claims.' It can be seen that this formulation does not require the notion of 'unpaid labour', but that it retains the idea of 'exploitation'. This in turn raises a certain problem of definition, since exploitation is ordinarily defined with reference to the idea of 'unpaid labour'. I simply suggest here that the question of 'payment' raises difficult semantic issues. By exploitation I mean that men try to make women work harder in order to increase their own prominence in the prestige-game of *moka*. The women are in that sense working to increase their husbands' status, but it is also true that in doing so they gain status for themselves. A wife who produces many pigs and is consulted carefully by her husband is invariably known as a 'big-woman' just as the husband may be referred to as a 'big-man'. There is no objective measurement of 'prestige', of course, but there is a rough relative ranking of men which is not so elaborate that one could call it a hierarchy. Women are not ranked in this way at all, and calling them 'big-women' is as much a matter of courtesy and appreciation for their work as it is an attribution of a status-grade in the *moka* as such.

Althusser's highly elaborate structuralist version of Marx's theory of economic determination gives a kind of metaphysical primacy to the structure as a whole. I am not concerned with Althusser's ideas on knowledge-production and theoretical practice but only with his theory of what is determinant within a mode of production, seen as a combination of technical and social relations of production and their associated ideological superstructures. In his formulation there is both an overall 'overdetermination' and a 'determination in the last instance' (Callinicos 1982: 60). The economy determines in the last instance only when other factors are set in the same direction as it itself is, and factors on the ideological level are not just passive reflections of the ineluctable development of productive forces. 'From the first moment to the last, the lonely hour of the last instance never comes.' Moreover, each practice constituting the social whole has its own 'peculiar time and history' (Callinicos 1982: 60, 64).

'Overdetermination' therefore refers to 'the structure as a whole', and the idea is that multiple elements combine to make the society what it is. This would be pure functionalism, were the vocabulary not also Marxist and concerned with contradiction and change. Althusser too so weakens the idea of the 'last instance' that it is almost lost from sight. Godelier's formula is not quite the same. He allows determining force to other elements *only if* they also function as relations of production. Yet this, too, gives wide latitude. If the *moka* in Hagen can be seen simply as a 'relation of production', it is apparent that almost any dominant institution in a society could also be seen as such, because such institutions invariably impinge strongly on the sphere of production. Further, since the *moka* has so many links with other social activities, to say that it is a relation of production says little more than that the society determines itself. It is not at this metaphysical level that the neo-Marxist concepts give insight, but rather it is in terms of the way they direct our attention to problems such as 'Is there inequality/exploitation/domination? Exactly how is it sustained and does it change?'

A more lengthy discussion of this problem is not needed here, because there is an admirably lucid and balanced survey available in Kahn's and Llobera's book *The Anthropology of Pre-capitalist Societies* (1981), especially in Joel Kahn's essay on 'Marxist Anthropology and Segmentary Societies' in that volume (pp. 57–88). Kahn examines each of the French neo-Marxist writers' contributions in turn, and concludes: 'All the Marxist writers on the lineage mode of production reject the vulgar formulations of some earlier Marxists. Rather, they all stress the distinctiveness of lineage societies, and hence the inapplicability of any general law of determination to the traditional object of anthropology.'

Essentially the same conclusion is reached by Maurice Bloch. After an admirably tense and lucid exposition of the ideas of Suret-Canale, Meillassoux, Terray, Rey, and Godelier, he writes that a Marxist anthropology is 'something to be created, not merely something to be revealed in the works of the founders' (1983: 172).

In such formulations we are very far from the simple application of the tenets of classical Marxism. My own formulation further recasts the debate by using a cross-cutting type of vocabulary, in which 'culture' is not synonymous with 'superstructure'. Yet neither do I suggest that we invert the traditional Marxist proposition and argue that culture is 'determinant'.

Rather, I suggest that there is in fact no one-to-one relationship between cultural and sociological factors. In many cases cultural features may be the 'signs' of underlying social processes, but this does not mean that these processes, as such, have 'determined' the cultural features, nor the reverse. In short, the *Zusammenhang* which undoubtedly exists is in my view more complex than is allowed by either Althusser's or Godelier's formulations. Godelier himself has in fact progressively refined his position further and further away from suggestions of 'vulgar materialism'.

Such a conclusion might be thought to entail analytical loss rather than a gain, since it replaces definite hypotheses with a 'no-hypothesis' position. In fact, however, this is not the intention. Intelligible relationships can be sought and stated in specific cases, but without committing ourselves in advance to the cranking of 'orreries' (see E. P. Thompson 1978).

It will be clear from my text that I have not plumped, in opposition to neo-Marxist approaches, for a purely individualistic version of exchange theory. Since individuals are indeed competitive and innovative in the Highlands, and since businessmen in particular show these qualities, it is obvious that a study of their behaviour and achievements should form an important part of the study of social change. I have already published a paper along these lines (A. J. Strathern 1972) but have not made a wider investigation of the activities of entrepreneurs at large. Such a study therefore remains to be done. My focus here is on a comparison and explanation of the main trends of change in two different societies, and for this a structurally-oriented framework is more suitable.

The Highlands peoples belong to Papua New Guinea and to the wider region of Melanesia which includes countries such as the Solomon Islands, Vanuatu (New Hebrides), and New Caledonia. Although their direct history of contact with Europeans is relatively brief, they obviously cannot be set up entirely as a 'special case' within this region, nor can we argue that outside influences had no effect on them prior to colonial penetration in the 1930s. The chief agricultural crop in the area, sweet potato, was probably introduced within the last three hundred years or so from South-East Asia, and whether in revolutionary or evolutionary terms it had definite effects on the structure of Highlands societies (see Brookfield and White 1968; Watson 1965; Golson 1981, 1982). Pearl shells, also, with other forms of sea shells, were imported via traditional trade-routes to north and south, and rates of supply and demand for these were indicators of indigenous processes of change and development for hundreds of years before the 1930s. Nevertheless, a number of local factors did operate to push change in particular directions during the colonial and immediate post-colonial periods. These were: the short time into which many political and economic pressures were crammed; the initial use of shells as a means of pacification; and the swift establishment of coffee plantations and later smallholdings. Corresponding with these, we find that Highlanders attempt constantly to combine indigenous and introduced value-systems; that pacification was no more than 'skin deep' and that fighting still breaks out on an endemic basis; and that a relatively sudden access to wealth has seemingly brought about an efflorescence of exchange activities, masking the development of a class system largely constructed around capitalist relations of production.

These statements are highly condensed and require elaboration. They also select from the full picture of change certain matters of emphasis, and here it is fitting that I enter a caveat. My studies have been on an narrow front: for example, I have not made a close examination of the missions, nor have I worked directly in any of the Highlands towns; neither have I covered large numbers of local communities. As a counterbalance to these limitations, however, I have studied two different language areas, each with a distinctive form of society and history, and it is the contrast between these two which is intended as a check on over-generalization from the data-base on either one of them. These two peoples are the Melpa of Mt Hagen in the Western Highlands Province, and the Wiru speakers of Pangia district in the Southern Highlands. The Melpa are more numerous, perhaps numbering 80,000; they were contacted earlier, in 1933 by explorers; and they have a more complex emphasis on 'big-manship' and ceremonial exchange than the Wiru, as well as greater current access to cash incomes through the sale of coffee and vegetables. At the same time, they also show a greater stress on 'quasi-traditonal' activities, particularly through the incorporation of money and goods bought with money, into their exchanges. These two area case studies pose the problem of understanding variations in exchange practices in the Highlands, and also the question of differential trajectories of change in response to colonial administration. Answers to these questions must again rely on a combination of cultural and sociological analysis. A brief summary of my arguments has appeared earlier (A. J. Strathern 1982a); here, more detail will be given.

A preliminary sketch of basic social structure is necessary as a background to the discussion of social changes which follows. As it happens, distinctions between the Melpa and Wiru are very clear, although it has taken me some time to formulate these. For a number of years I tended to assume that there was more similarity between the two societies than is in fact the case. The reason was that my fieldwork with the Wiru followed immediately after I had completed two dissertations on Hagen society, and I was much influenced by the Hagen 'models' which I had constructed, even though in formal terms I was explicitly seeking comparisons and differences in the exchange systems of the two areas. I had developed the idea of 'finance' versus 'production' as a factor in differentiating Highlands societies, and chose to work in Wiru as it was a 'pig-killing' area rather than one in which *moka* exchange, with its financial manipulations, was practised (A. J. Strathern 1969). This approach was certainly borne out by the data which I collected, but what my sociological hypothesis had not prepared me for was the understanding of differences at the cultural level. These relate to ideas about the sexes, the meaning of exchange, the use of non-verbal versus verbal communication, and the codes employed in self-decoration. The first article in which I was able to place side by side sociological and cultural analysis was called 'Finance and Production Revisited', published in 1978.[1] In this I explained the set of structural contrasts surrounding the use of speech in Melpa and Wiru exchange festivals. These contrasts in turn had a crucial point of correspondence with the social structure, since they reflected a difference in marriage practices, whereby in Melpa marriage patterns are expected to tie in with political alliances, whereas in Wiru they are not.

Detailed information for these two areas has been obtained for only one major social group in each case: the Kawelka (or Kaulka) people among the Melpa, and the place Tunda among the Wiru, predominantly associated with the Peri people. There are considerable risks in using such data to generalize about much larger populations, probably some 80,000 for the Melpa and 18,000 for the Wiru. Nevertheless, my acquaintance with materials on other groups suggest that for broad purposes these two groups may be taken as *prima facie* examples of how groups in general are constituted. It would be a difficult, and very lengthy, task to undertake the ideal, that of investigating all the named social groups and their histories. For Hagen, however, there are numerous other ethnographic works; and for the Wiru, there is the PhD research carried out by Jeffrey Clark in Taguru (or Takuru) village, which is just outside of the ambit of Tunda's own alliances (Clark, in preparation 1982). With these provisos, then, I proceed to speak of 'the Melpa' and 'Wiru' (see *Maps 1* and *2*; see also Vicedom and Tischner 1943 – 48; Strauss and Tischner 1962; Brandewie 1981).

Students of Highlands social groups, as has been noted by others, have almost invariably identified the 'clan' as the basic social unit (de Lepervanche 1967 – 68). While such a label fits Melpa groups rather well, its application to the Wiru is more doubtful. The reasons for this appear to lie in different historical adaptations to the contingencies of warfare. In Melpa the social groups in general are larger and more numerous, and the clan is normatively expected to occupy a single territory and to practise exogamy, as well as acting as a definite group in warfare (in pre-contact times) and exchange (today). Clans therefore emerge ideologically as sets of men on their own ground, plus their in-married wives and their children. In Wiru there is a somewhat similar ideology but its realization in locality terms is different.

To use the original terminology invented by Hogbin and Wedgwood (1952 – 54) in Hagen localized groups are 'monocarpellary', whereas in Pangia they are 'multicarpellary'. But this formula also is potentially misleading. What it points to is the fact that the internal structure of groups within the wider political unit is more complicated in the case of the Wiru. The best way to indicate this is by an example. In the Tunda area, the people as a whole are known by the name Peri, and this refers to their political identity *vis-à-vis* other groups in surrounding villages. These in turn are sometimes referred to in similar manner. Thus Tunda people refer to those of Mamuane village, their enemies in warfare prior to pacification, as the Kaimari. Most often the word *ali*, 'man' or 'men', is added to indicate that the speaker is thinking of these names as referring to groups of men linked by the name itself. But they may also use the locality name, e.g. *Tunda ali*, *Mamuane ali*, with the same meaning. The significance of these usages is always in the first place political. Looking below the level of their 'big names', we find both that the large locality or parish is in fact split into a number of big hamlets or villages, and that the Peri group contains within it many sub-groups, but not all linked by a single myth of descent or a single segmentary structure corresponding with such a myth. There is a broad

Map 1 Hagen and surrounding areas

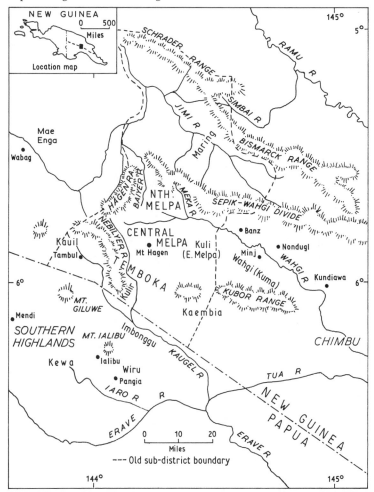

Source: A. Strathern, *The Rope of Moka.* Cambridge University Press, 1977.

structure of political relationships between the member groups within the Peri complex, but this cannot be seen simply as a precipitate of descent nor is it represented as such by the people themselves. Instead it is presented as what it is, a set of alliances based on historical events, although the events themselves are given a mythological character.

Map 2 Pangia District, Southern Highlands Province

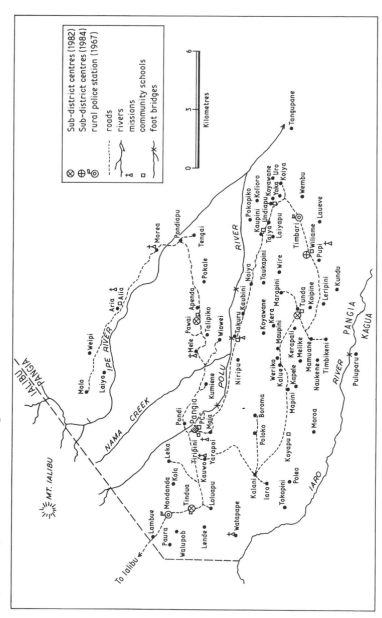

Source: Dr Sheldon Weeks, Education Research Unit, University of Papua New Guinea.

The two main political blocs in the Tunda area are the Windiperi and Angaliri pair and the Leonoperi and Waluperi pair. Each of these is a definite social group, exogamous, and with at least a notional idea of descent from a single man. But there is no overall idea that a single named ancestor founded all these Peri sub-groups. Moreover, this pattern of $2 + 2 = 4$, which is highly reminiscent of the models of Hagen warfare that I developed when writing about the relationship of exchange to warfare there (A. J. Strathern 1971b: Chapter 4), leaves out a number of important facts. The first is that two of the component villages in the area contain groups which politically identify with the Peri as a whole but are avowedly also splinters from other large named categories co-ordinate with the Peri, whose men at some stage in the past lived there. The main village associated with Tunda in this way in 1967 was Kerepali, and its people could be placed together by Tunda residents as *Lombo Peri*, or the Peri of the bush place Lombo. 'Peri' itself is the name of a large dispersed category. Some of its people are to be found near to Ialibu, others again in the Kagua District at Koiro village, where some say the name originated. The point here is not to reconstruct the history of the Peri in detail, but merely to indicate that the name as such has two overlapping but distinct referents: one is the political unit centering around Tunda, and the other the dispersed category itself. It is the latter that may be properly termed a phratry as such. The former sense of the term, however, refers to neither a clan (since the Peri as a whole are not exogamous) nor to a phratry (since it signifies only a section of the wider phratry). A term is needed for this phenomenon, and I call it 'the dominant name', a cumbersome usage, but one that is necessary in order to avoid confusion. The extent to which a single 'name' dominates in other political confederations based on different villages may well vary.[2] Tunda people, however, do use this idiom in speaking of others, particularly their enemies. Thus, the Mamuane folk are *Kaimari ali*, the Kalue people *Tawindi ali*. Further, the extent to which such a 'big name' is in fact dispersed among different villages also varies. Kaimari people are found in Tunda itself, as well as in Mamuane, for example, but there are no Peri in Mamuane. Further, the status of the name changes when its members are incorporated into a village other than one where they are dominant. They are categorized as *pirikanango* or *awiranango*, those who 'live with' or came as 'refugees' to be with the *tapinango* or original occupants. They do not suffer any jural disabilities in terms of land rights or the right to speak on local issues, but it is the case that they usually do

not have the numbers to be influential in local politics and, politically
speaking, they become partly merged with those who bear the dominant name itself. In all cases close ties of intermarriage bind them to
one of the main groups. But, and this is the difference between 'incorporation' in Melpa and Wiru, they retain their own original big name'
and this continues to be transmitted. In this sense, therefore, agnation
is always preserved in Wiru.

The reason for this has to do not with an absolute value placed on
agnation as such, but with matrilateral payments (see Harrison 1982 on
a Sepik village). Such payments are due to maternal kin, and one's
agnatic line cannot therefore be merged with theirs, even if one is living
with them. In Hagen, payments of this kind are also made, but their
significance is much greater in Wiru social structure. A kind of locality
alliance also links the main segments of the Peri. Thus Waluperi and
Leonoperi, who form a pair, do not share a single ancestor, but their
ancestors are said to have met and made friends. The same is true of
Windiperi and Angaliri, but in this case there is a further twist, since
Angaliri are avowedly of a different 'big name' from elsewhere (the
Ialibu area, in fact, near to Lake Mbuna), and when they first came they
spoke only Ialibu talk, which is related to Melpa. Their ancestors made
friends with the Peri at the place Windi (hence 'Windiperi'), and so
they settled down. Here is an example, then, of a different 'big name'
group becoming fully integrated with the *tapinango*.[3] Yet their name
itself records that there is a difference, and in fact their political stance
tends also to be independent, without full allegiance to either Windiperi or to the other pair of groups.

In Melpa similar processes, whereby groups have joined with others,
have certainly occurred, and in certain regards, e.g. marriage rules,
these may maintain some of their earlier identity. But in general they
are more tightly locked into the segmentary group structures. Individuals who join from other groups are very quickly incorporated (as they
are among the neighbouring mid-Wahgi people), and as the rules of
membership are filiative rather than dependent on descent, so a man
who belongs as a member via a female link such as the mother, has
children who are themselves accepted as members through their father.
It does happen, however, that a whole group segment may develop
from such a process and in time the segment as a whole will become
known as 'children of the woman' (*amb-nt-mei*). This is the reverse of
the normal process whereby segments are named as the shoots (*-mbo*)
of an in-marrying woman of a certain tribe who came to a male ancestor.

In Wiru there is no such commemoration of in-marriage and no equivalent of the Melpa *amb-nt-mei / wuö-nt-mei* distinction. Agnates remain as they are; cognates are not converted into agnates. On the other hand men can and do move from one place to another acquiring a new political identity via their residence and participation in pig-kills and assuming in some contexts the 'big name' which is dominant in that locality. But their original agnatic identity always *also* remains, underneath this political level. Even if a person is taken in by his mother's people, he will still make payments to them 'for his skin' at times in his lifetime and he may return to his agnates at a later stage (A. J. Strathern 1971a, 1982b).

Once again, we should not see these patterns as reflecting fundamentally different ideas about descent in itself, but rather as a product of the articulation of the ties of descent, locality, and intermarriage. Among the Melpa, descent and locality become fused and the descent idiom acquires structural salience. The local descent groups are then seen to be allied and/or opposed, and the more the alliance aspect is stressed the more it is linked to the facts of intermarriage between the whole groups concerned. These in turn are strengthened by repeated *moka* exchanges over time. The affinal bonds generated by marriage thus have a formal role to play in binding together separate clan communities and there is no in-marriage within the clan, except in cases where non-agnates are involved and the aim is to tie them strongly to the clan by a link of this kind. In the Wiru case, the political locality, identified with a village name, is also identified with a level higher than the exogamous unit. There is considerable intermarriage both within and outside this locality and, in the Peri case at any rate, there is no observable or stated preference for marrying with political allies. Yet the most important exchanges are with those linked by such marriages, so that there is a disjunction between exchanges at this level and political alliance.

In an account of this kind, there is some danger of producing a description in which the time reference is mixed, thereby setting up a false framework. I do not really know how exchanges worked in the past during the times of warfare among the Wiru, since I was not there to see at the time. It is possible that gifts were not made in the past to affines when these were from enemy groups. But if so, it is hard to imagine how the marriages themselves took place other than by capture (a small number were in fact of this type), and the Wiru ideology of giving to maternal kin is so strong that it is impossible, in my view, to conceive of it as a purely post-1960 phenomenon. Life-history materials in any case indicate that matrilateral payments were made at all times in the remembered past.

The other two spheres in which contrasts between the Melpa and Wiru show are in the development of big-manship and in the way the roles of the sexes are seen. There are Wiru big-men, known as *kamoango*, but their power and influence seems in no way to have reached that of big-men in the central Hagen area. Again, there are historical problems because the Wiru system had been strongly affected by recent changes when I first studied it in 1967. But the weight of evidence shows that the above observation is basically correct. Big-men did not monopolize valuables in the past; no stories of despots were told; polygynists had no more than three wives at a given time; there are no mechanisms of increment or long, worked-out chain structures of exchange partnerships in Wiru as there are among Melpa. All these points indicate the same thing: that big-manship had not 'taken off' among the Wiru. Even the term *kamo* means 'white clay', the clay put on for mourning when maternal kin come and ask for payments, and this suggests that a *kamo-ango* is still locked into the affinal-matrilateral nexus of gifts.

Finally, since the big-man concept is not so highly developed, here the overall structural inequality between the sexes is not as stressed. There are two elements to this in Highlands societies. One is the fact of normative virilocality: a woman leaves her ground and goes to the man's ground, so that she is already in a sense 'alienated'. But this is much modified among the Wiru, where marriage within the political locality is common. Nevertheless, it is a structural fact. The other element is the peculiar Hagen linking of prestige / rubbishness with male / female categories. This association is distinctly muted among the Wiru. For the Wiru, also, it seems that the two sexes are not seen as different in a secure and absolute sense, as they are in Hagen (M. Strathern 1982). The sexes can 'take each other's place'. Women are not just 'in between' sets of men, as they are in Hagen. The sexes are said to 'make' each other in sexual intercourse (*anume ne tuku*, 'I am making you', 'I am doing it to you'), whereas in Hagen it is a matter of a man 'striking' a woman with his penis as he might with a spear (*wuö rui* means 'to kill a man', *amb rui* ordinarily means 'to have intercourse with' a woman). The term in Wiru for a married pair rolls the sexes together: *andonora*, which looks like a conflation of *andene* = penis and *andu* = breast, + *ra* = two. And the term for changing identity suggests that identity is something 'built' or 'constructed' (*lariko*) rather than something 'planted' (*rökli*), as in Melpa. At the same time male ideology certainly does exist among the

Wiru. Women themselves use phrases which attest to the idea of male strength and female weakness, but women are also very quick to tell men that they are actually 'women' (*ne aroa tandeko*), so turning the ideology back against men. In both places men also claim they wish to have sons rather than daughters, or at any rate they want their wives to bear sons first and daughters later, because these sons will take their place. For the Wiru there is some slight evidence, even, of female infanticide (a practice which would help control population density). This is surprising, since daughters are a road for exchanges, and such exchanges are a fundamental part of the reproduction of society.

These contrasts in structure between the two societies are all of some relevance to the picture of recent social changes. Basic social structure as such does not appear to have been altered greatly in either area, so that one has to think of it as an element of continuity while considering the factors of change. The most obvious importance resides at the political level. Wiru big-manship was not and is not as highly developed as in Hagen. At the same time, as I have already argued (A. J. Strathern 1982a), the Wiru were faced with swift and many-faceted influences from Europeans at a late stage in colonial history, whereas in Hagen the effects of colonialism were felt more gradually, and the first phase, as among the Siane of the Eastern Highlands (Salisbury 1962) actually produced a kind of 'boom' in big-manship which the Wiru never experienced. I shall return to this comparison with the Siane in the final chapter. I will begin with a discussion of pacification and its aftermath, followed by a chapter on the mission activities which have been particularly crucial as agencies of social change in Pangia.

Notes

1 This article was written in April 1977, and interestingly enough, it coincided with a severe bout of malaria (for a parallel see Wagner 1967: Introduction).
2 The 'big name' as such has also come to have political significance in post-contact times, as it has in Hagen. This was shown in the 1982 national elections, when one candidate secured the votes of the members of his dispersed phratry throughout the Wiru area: Robert Paia, who obtained the votes of the Ieneperi.
3 This story runs as follows: Windi Piko had no wife and lived by himself. The Angaliri came from the river Anga at Mbuna. They quarrelled over the stomach of a cooked cassowary bird and some migrated down into Wiru, these are the descendants of Pepo. Windi Piko took Pepo in as a friend, and Pepo gave him a girl of the Makari phratry. Piko married her and had sons. Since that time Angaliri and Windiperi do not intermarry.

2 Pacification

The apparent ease with which the warlike societies of the Highlands were pacified in the 1930s and 1940s has been matched in the 1970s and early 1980s with an equally speedy reversion to forcible methods of dealing with disputes; and this despite an increasingly elaborate array of police and court officials whose function it is to contain such violence. Why is this so?

The possible answers to this question are multifarious. The two most popular ones current among academics and government officials are of sharply different kinds. In one view, the fighting is a straight-out reversion to traditional ways of handling quarrels, adopted because the introduced institutions have not greatly altered the people's way of thinking. This is therefore, in essence, a mentalist explanation. In the other main view, *per contra*, the fighting is seen as basically a new phenomenon, produced through the strains caused by economic development, and covertly acting as a protest against the new class inequalities which are rapidly emerging. This is clearly a materialist explanation. Both explanations are too extreme. But what we need to decide is in which sense is fighting a reversion and in which is it new?

One way into the problem has been to stress the significance of land and shortage of land. Meggitt, for example, has argued both that land is a supreme value to the Mae-Enga people, and that the renewed fighting in Enga Province has resulted from an exacerbation of land problems, caused by the freezing of boundaries, the frustrations of litigation, increase in populations, and the use of land for cash as well as subsistence cropping. Meggitt's earlier hypothesis on Mae society was in the same vein, that the degree of effective patrilineality and patri-locality in Highlands social groups varies with the amount of pressure on available agrarian resources (Meggitt 1965, 1977; Rodman and Cooper 1979). The 'supreme value' of land here is simply its capacity to sustain human life; but one must note that the Mae are also among those Highlands peoples who raise large numbers of pigs for ceremonial exchanges, and pig herds therefore represent a value added to that of subsistence itself, the value of prestige.

The argument can be taken a step further. Prestige is itself not simply an immaterial idea. It belongs to a nexus in which symbolic values and material factors are continuously linked. A linear account of how social practices may have developed suffers from the difficulty of choosing a starting point from which to 'derive' other factors – the same difficulty attended the development of generative models of society as proposed by Frederik Barth in the 1960s (Barth 1966). With-out trying to reconstruct a pseudo-history of how Enga society may have developed, one can at any rate point out that the value placed on pigs goes well beyond any nutritional concern or requirements. Whenever Highlands populations have taken up the intensive rearing of pigs, this certainly has had a transforming influence on their social system. But each cultural step, linked with new social practices, is linked also to the cultural past. Pigs have been in the Highlands for a long time, perhaps as long as 10,000 years, and the *choice* made by Enga people to intensify pig rearing was made on the basis of the pig's existing religious and political significance in their area. If this is so, the 'pressure on agrarian resources' is a product of such historial choices and cultural values, and not just an automatic demographic phenomenon (see Morren 1977).

The same is true of fighting as a method of handling land disputes. The Enga and other Highlanders were accustomed to fighting over land boundaries, and their traditions of doing so have not been broken or forgotten. Cultural elements are therefore involved. Nevertheless, there *was* a period of pacification, during which both government and

missions urged people to give up fighting. The people, acting ration-
ally, complied, first because of the threat of force and second because of
the apparent benefits promised. One very important cultural element
involved in this process in the Hagen area was the fact that Europeans
were interpreted as manifestations of light-skinned sky beings considered to be the ultimate source behind the power of local social
groups to reproduce themselves. The explorers were associated with the
sky since they came with assistance from light aircraft; they were
certainly light-skinned, and, finally, they brought with them 'red'
coloured wealth in the form of cloth and pearl shells as well as steel axes
and knives (Strauss 1962: Chapter 14). All accounts of the first meetings with Europeans stress how amazed and delighted Hagen men were
to discover that the intruders carried these coveted technological and
'political' objects with them and were prepared to part with them in
return for food and labour. In addition, Hageners stood in awe of these
incomers, because they regarded them as having supernatural power,
an idea reinforced by the material power of their axes and guns. In the
Pangia area, this cultural aspect of the early encounters was modified,
first by the fact that steel tools had penetrated into the area well before
Europeans actually arrived in the 1950s, and second by the policy then
in operation to get the local people involved in the cash economy as
quickly as possible, and thus away from the 'pearl shell standard'. In
the slightly longer run, the effect of this was the opposite. In Hagen,
pearl shells became too numerous, lost their value, and went out of
fashion, to be replaced both symbolically and practically by cash;
whereas in Pangia the shells continue in fact to be used along with cash,
pork, and live pigs as items for exchange. These shells are all still
individually named, and the paths of exchange along which they come
into an individual's hands are generally well known.

In Pangia also Europeans were initially assigned to a spirit category.
They were spoken of as *uele nekenea* 'coming along the water-courses'.
This phrase likens, if not equates, them with the ghosts of the dead
who travel in this way out of and back into local group territories. All
their goods and wealth were held to have come by the same route, and
their arrival was also in some way conflated with the myth of the Female
Spirit, a goddess known in the neighbouring Mendi and Enga areas as
well as northwards, in Mount Hagen. A white woman known as *Mis
Aroa* (i.e. Mrs Woman) was said to be trying to make her way into
Pangia, but was stumbling on the rocky limestone paths. Songs were
sung for her which were influenced by half-heard versions of mission

hymns, requesting her to come. The actual Female Spirit cult, *Aroa Ipono*, had been introduced into Pangia by ritual specialists from the Kewa-speaking area, flanking the Wiru speakers of Pangia on their north-west; this was within living memory according to senior men in 1967. But the story of the *Mis Aroa* is reminiscent of the *Sundo Owil* story known in Mendi, and this in turn is a variant of the Female Spirit myth (Mawe 1982). The general point here is that one way or another Europeans were associated with existing categories of spirit entities. The link with water-courses also potentially compares them with the wild water-spirit *Uelali*, thought of in Wiru as a dangerous agent of sickness and death. There can be little doubt that the apparent success that small numbers of white people had in swiftly 'pacifying' populations who were engaged in chronic fighting, had much to do, throughout the Highlands, with the fact that they brought steel tools and valuable shells, *and* also that they were credited with being the 'origin-people' (in Melpa *pukl-wamb* the 'true owners') of these items. In Melpa steel goods were all classified as 'spirit' items, thus *kor rui* 'spirit axe', *kor wambnga kui tina* 'white marsupial fur of the spirit people', a term for cotton cloth. In Wiru, stone axes were called *tipalira*; the steel version is named *tue*, which seems related to the Melpa *rui*, and is distinguished from the term for 'dog' only by a rising tone on its first syllable as opposed to a falling one. Perhaps the near-homonym occurred as an accidental by-product of the recent borrowing of the term from areas to the north where Europeans were established in numbers long before they arrived in Pangia.

These cognitive aspects of early contacts are not presented with the intention of denying the material side of the encounter. The point is rather that the cognitive and material aspects are not separate. In both Hagen and Pangia, as elsewhere in the Highlands, the fact that Europeans carried tools, valuables, and guns simply pointed to the 'fact' that they were spirit beings, coming from the sources of such things. Myths about the 'sources' of crops, wealth, and social customs are common in Melanesia. These are not thought of simply as origin points *in* linear time. They remain the true sources *over* time, and sometimes access to them is blocked and the flow of 'values' has to be re-stimulated by ritual (Harrison 1982). A ritual attitude towards Europeans was therefore predictable. It is clear that some people were nevertheless tempted to attack the explorers, to seize their wealth, and were repulsed by force where they did not succeed. Some died and others were maimed in these contests. Their names and histories were preserved, along with the names of those who used the opposite technique of making friends with these new spirit creatures. Those who did this were in fact regarded as the more daring, since they were likely to be eaten at any moment, according to local belief. The newcomers were thought to take some of their shell wealth out of their own anuses, another act reminiscent of the doings of creator heroes in mythology (and of course entailing a piece of symbolism with a familiar Freudian touch to it). This was how the Europeans' pockets were interpreted, since their trousers were seen as a part of their skin itself. If one asks, therefore, whether the Highlanders were pacified by the use of force, one must answer that force was certainly an element, but it acquired further significance from the wider context of cognition into which it was set. The same background also explains why missions everywhere success- fully established themselves in the wake of the first explorers and government officers.

Similar points apply to the material transactions between the in- comers and the local people. Shells established Europeans as worth befriending. Their actual use had a number of objective effects, of which the most prominent were that they cross-cut the normal rules of exchange, in which food crops were not directly transacted for shell wealth, thus introducing a short circuit in the acquisition of wealth. Second, their increasing numbers gradually forced the exchange value of the shells down, at least in Hagen. These were facts not planned or even 'cognized' by the people, and they helped to produce the colonial version of society which existed in the 1960s when I first did fieldwork. With them we move back into 'sociology' or 'unintended results of action'. As Ian Hughes has argued (1978), at a further level of analysis away from the 'cognized model', it is also possible to argue that the exchange of food for wealth created a sense of dependency on the part of the Highlands populations, which later resulted in their opposition to the removal of Australian rule in the early 1970s. This was done on the grounds that the white men were the true owners of wealth and knowledge, and if the existing colonial hierarchy were abolished, wealth would no longer flow from them. Highlanders later discovered that matters were more complicated than this. The change in government did not mean that Europeans disappeared altogether; although many went, others came. If anything, business activity accelerated, as both Highlanders and Europeans consolidated and expanded their activities.

Another fear, however, which was expressed in the 1970s, did prove realistic. This was that the fragile basis of pacification would collapse with the ending of the regime of generalist colonial administration through government officers known as kiaps (from German *Kapitan*, via Pidgin English). In Hagen a spectacular form of pacification and expansion of exchange was followed, as also in the Enga and Chimbu (Simbu) Provinces, by an equally startling resumption of inter-group hostilities which still persists. Reasons developed as to why a particular area or province of the Highlands has not yet experienced a resurgence of violent action have proved strictly temporary: understanding the dynamics of processes in time is difficult. During the 1970s it was apparent that the Eastern Highlands Province was not suffering from the same problems of 'law and order' as were being dramatically experienced in three of the provinces to its west within the Highlands region. This appeared paradoxical from one point of view, since it was these Eastern Highlands societies in which the traditions of leadership were most closely tied up with prowess in warfare, whereas to the west there was a greater emphasis on leadership through exchange along the lines which became established as the 'big-man' model. Any hypothesis which simply looked on contemporary fighting as a reversion to the past would have to cope with this paradox. At the time I relied upon the argument that the traditional structuring of leadership in the Eastern Highlands had collapsed, owing to early pacification and the banning of male initiation cults by missionaries. The people were also introduced to coffee-growing as a business activity from the early 1950s, and made a rapid switch from pearl shells to cash during the 1960s. Preoccupied with business, they turned towards the new structures and opportunities offered by the Administration. By contrast, in the Western Highlands, including Hagen, the practices of traditional-style leadership were not destroyed, but in a sense enhanced, by the arrival of the Europeans. The competition for positions of big-manship was increased, ceremonies were staged more frequently and an ideology of paying for past killings was vigorously promulgated by men who gained access to the new supplies of shell wealth. At the same time, exchange kept alive not only the good relationships between groups but also memories of their past hostilities. The oral history of politics was preserved, developed, and constantly brought into play. Moreover, the elaborate exchanges themselves produced new strains between groups and individuals, both when one group eclipsed another and when the opposite occurred through a group reneging on its obligations. In this way the ground was laid for the resumption, from time to time, of hostilities, especially since exchange had been set up between groups that did not previously have strong alliances. Road accidents, land disputes, and accusations of sorcery provided the immediate reasons for suspicion and violent revenge. Inflated demands for compensation further increased tensions.

These observations are adequate as far as they go. But it has to be recognized that certain underlying factors have been at work throughout the Highlands region, and that these conduce towards aggressive physical action as a means of settling disputes. That this is so is apparent from the fact that in 1981 and 1982 the Eastern Highlands had its share of violence and inter-group fighting; one part of the Western Highlands, Dei Council, which remained free of large, overt inter-group confrontations during the 1970s, also experienced problems in 1982. These factors may be listed as: (1) in *all* areas the traditions of fighting remain alive, even if dormant; (2) in all areas new class inequalities are gradually eating into community life; (3) in all areas, land has become a means of earning a cash income, and this is so regardless of whether there is an 'objective' land shortage or not; and (4) in all areas the scale of social relations has altered to a point where the people cannot control the activities of their leaders. In the Eastern Highlands, for example, opposition to the Provincial Government's proposed retail sales tax was met by the Premier, Mr James Yanepa, saying flatly that he is the government and the decision will not be changed. The fact that 1982 was a general election year is also not to be discounted.[1]

In Dei Council inter-group issues emerged between the Kombukla, the Roklaka, and the Römndi tribes, and these were undoubtedly exacerbated by the state of tension produced by the elections. Roklaka and Römndi were likely to support a single candidate against two standing from Kombukla. The specific causes of fighting were to do with land. A group from the Minembi tribe (paired with Kombukla) had fought with a Römndi clan. One day a Römndi driver saw a number of Minembi enemies waiting beside the road. Allegedly, he deliberately drove his bus at them, but they quickly scattered, having exposed a Kombukla leader. This man had rather weak knees and was slow in rising. The driver braked and swerved but still knocked him over. He was concussed and suffered brain damage. The Römndi paid a sum variously estimated at K3,000 and K5,000 to his relatives, with a promise of more should he die, but feelings still ran strong. The Roklaka for their part had objected to a land deal in which a Kombukla businessman was granted a development lease over some 3,000 hectares

of government land which included a part to which the Roklaka themselves held traditional claims. Quarrels and injuries resulted, culminat-
ing in a battle in which one Roklaka man was killed. It was said that he
had flicked his tongue between his lips in scorn of his assailants, an
action that arouses the anger of the ghosts who watch over fighting,
who guided the enemy's spears to him. Several Kombukla men suffered arrow wounds. The Roklaka swore that the Kombukla would not
visit Hagen town for the next five years, since they would guard the
road into it and kill any Kombukla man who tried to travel there. A
Kombukla woman married into the Kawelka tribe was also raped and
her husband harassed as they were walking along the road one evening.
The Kawelka leader, Ongka, demanded compensation for this, since
wives are married into their husband's groups, and the Kawelka had no
part in the dispute. A Kawelka man commented to me, 'We used to say
that we had no trouble in Dei Council, but now look at all this!' The
Dei people had been saying that by contrast with themselves the Mul
Council folk were always in strife, and indeed earlier in 1982 the
Kumndi group in Mul had been involved in large-scale fighting and
subsequent massive compensation payments. Dei folk even said they
wanted no more intermarriage with Mul, because the incoming Mul
women would bring their quarrelsome ways with them. This attitude
undoubtedly went back to a much earlier pair of events in which a Mul
driver was killed inside Dei. The Dei MP, Parua-Kuri, was subsequently
violently attacked in an attempted revenge, despite the fact that compensation had long since been paid. The Mul group involved in this
case were the Nengka Kuklanggil clan, and these in turn have links
with the Römndi and the Roklaka, as traditional members of the
Pipilika phratry. The Pipilika clans were formed into a Development
Association, which acts in competition with another such association,
Welyi-Kuta, whose core consists of a Kombukla alliance with the Welyi
tribe. The two Associations in the past contested the right to take over
ownership of Gumanch Plantation, the largest coffee plantation in the
Western Highlands Province; Pipilika gained it.

These examples show the ramifications of disputes in which issues to
do with the commercial exploitation of land are becoming increasingly
important. The whole province is now being 'carved' into areas owned
by indigenous business groups and individuals. This will lead to a new
pattern of inequality based directly on capital assets, and because each
of these groups is based on a collocation of traditional and 'neo-
traditional' ties the potential for inter-group conflict will remain. It is

not surprising that the most prominent businessmen also tend to support those political parties which stand for a combination of 'law and order' and 'commercial enterprise'. The connection between these two planks of the political platform is clear.

Two matters remain to be discussed: pacification in Pangia and administrative change. The two are connected. In the early 1970s it was often stated that one of the main reasons for the outbreak of intergroup fights was the erosion of the system of 'hard-fisted' administration by generalist patrol officers, who originally held both police and magisterial powers. These men were able to act as judge, gaoler, and jury in matters involving breaches of Native Regulations, and on their patrols could mete out swift punishment to offenders, and prevent small disputes from escalating. Regular patrolling was encouraged by the senior staff in the Native Administration, and it was seen as a means to promotion. Young kiaps, recruited mostly from Australia, developed a strong sub-culture of attitudes reinforcing their abrupt and decisive ways of dealing with the people, whom they referred to as 'the kanakas' and 'orly'. (The latter was from the Pidgin phrase *oli*, meaning 'they'. This last was a kiap's 'in' joke, since whenever kiaps asked who was responsible for doing something wrong, the reply was always that 'they' did it.) The Highlands provided a context in which this particular variant of Australian culture was able to flourish to a high degree, and it was dominant in the late 1950s and early 1960s when pacification took place in Pangia.

The area had no direct experience of the earlier pioneer patrolling of the 1930s, although the people had often seen planes travelling in the sky and spoke of them as coming from Murumba, a version of 'Moresby', the capital city, to the south. Stations were set up at Mendi and Ialibu, and occasional patrols passed through the Wiru people's territory in search of murderers during the 1950s. Medical patrols followed, and the Pangia station was set up in 1960. By this time, several prominent leaders had already been to Ialibu, north of Pangia, and had received badges as *tultuls*. They and their groups next participated in the building of a link road between Ialibu and Pangia stations. This was a familiar Administration strategy, designed to maximize labour at the same time as introducing newly-administered peoples to others with earlier experience of the colonial system. Such contacts could result in new social ties: in Hagen Tipuka-Kawelka men went to construct the Baiger River Gorge road with Kumndi men, and came back with some Kumndi wives given to them in appreciation of their assistance.

The first kiaps at Pangia held firmly to the accepted ethic of patrolling, plus exhorting the people to accept the Administration way of doing things. They were career officers: one later became an Assistant District Commissioner, and the other a District Court Magistrate (Mr Peter Barber and Mr Brian O'Neill, respectively). Pacification was not difficult, even though wars were still being fought in the 1950s. The Wiru are not short of agricultural land, although disputes over land are endemic and food shortages are by no means unknown. Minor encouragement was given to groups to pay compensation for killings; disputed land areas were ordered not to be used by contending groups. People had already heard stories of what the white men brought with them and this was their biggest incentive to comply with what the newcomers wanted. Pangia airstrip was constructed with massive communal labour as a means of access to the 'cargo' of goods which was to come.

Two features of this process stand out as different from the earlier Hagen experience of the 1930s and 1940s. First, in Hagen, the incomers were entirely new, unheralded except by a few stray pieces of cloth and steel. In Pangia, by contrast, a good deal of knowledge had filtered through from Hagen and Ialibu by the time that the government station was set up. The people were prepared for the takeover, and what they wanted from the start was not merely shells, but the complete 'development package'. What they got was part of the 'colonial package'. They received the attentions of four different missions: the Evangelical Bible Mission, the Wesleyans, the Catholics, and the Lutherans. In addition, a Summer Institute linguist established himself and his family in a village a few miles from the station.[2] Whatever indigenous categories the newcomers were placed into these, as noted earlier, were quickly overlain or supplanted by the ideologies put forward by the missionaries themselves. While these usually thought of themselves as freeing the people from fear of pagan spirits, in fact they created a great deal of fear themselves, with their strange stories of life after death and heaven and hell. There is little doubt that the pacification of Pangia was facilitated by this fear in a way which did not happen in Hagen.

The second difference is one I have already noted. Pearl shells were brought in by the Administration, but in nothing like the quantities that had poured into Hagen from the 1930s through to the 1950s, and some of which had probably found their way into the Southern Highlands. The people already knew of many other things the white men had.

The Administration was committed to an accelerated programme of introduced change in which pearl shells were to be replaced with cash as quickly as possible and labourers recruited to go to coastal plantations under the Highlands Labour Scheme. There was, therefore, no period of efflorescence of the local exchange system in association with pacification. Leaders were encouraged to identify quickly with Administration needs and demands, and were given little spare time in which to expand their traditional bases of strength. At the same time, for the first few years little cash came into the area. The overall effect was to depress the already muted version of big-manship which the Pangia people had, and to concentrate the people's attention on achieving prominence through working with the Administration and/or missions. In 1967, when I first went there, Pangia seemed, if anything, more transformed than Mount Hagen, despite only seven years of direct administration. Correspondingly, through to the time of self-government in 1973, Pangia people were alarmed and shocked to hear of the extent to which Hagen people were prepared to break, challenge, or bypass the white man's law. This knowledge in itself probably forced them to rethink their own understanding of their situation. They were sure that if anyone tried to fight in Pangia as people did in Hagen, they would undoubtedly all be thrown in gaol, whereas somehow in Hagen this seemed not to happen.

The reason was simple: the Pangia people were still in the first stages of regarding Europeans with a mixture of awe and fear, and the kiap system was still strong in the Southern Highlands right through to the time of Independence in 1975, whereas in Hagen very considerable modifications had already taken place. Police powers had been separated from those of kiaps, who no longer commanded their own police; local courts were set up with specialist magistrates, replacing the Courts of Native Affairs previously run by kiaps. Further, of course, many people were now literate and had been to coastal towns, so that they stood much less in awe of Europeans than before. No kiap by then dared to strike people, or make them eat raw lizards, or force them to dig large holes as compulsory labour and then make them sleep in these as a means of confining them – all of which were done at different places in the Western Highlands in the 1940s and 1950s.

Since 1977 patrolling by kiaps in Pangia has also decreased. The station is now run by a District Manager, equivalent to the old rank of District Officer or Assistant District Commissioner. The same division of powers in regard to law and order exists as that in Hagen. However, to date serious inter-group fighting has not taken place. Severe rivalries have rather coalesced around aspiring politicians, and in the 1982 election campaign at least one serious fracas occurred between supporters of the sitting MP and one of his main opponents, a recent university graduate. The reasons for this pattern will be examined again, after Wiru social structure has been given more consideration. Here, it remains to evaluate the general argument that administrative changes contributed to the breakdown of law and order in Hagen.

In place of the dominant role played by generalist field officers, the following structures were set up. (1) A separate police hierarchy, with urban and rural zones. The police have no particular day-to-day communication with provincial officials, and police work remains a national function, not one which has been devolved to the province level. (2) A separate official court hierarchy, with Local and District Court magistrates. These may also serve in special Land Courts, for which there is particular legislation, and in courts set up to deal with tribal fighting. (3) Village Courts, with their own magistrates and Peace Officers, chosen from among local people. These courts were designed to put more power back into the hands of the people. In practice they have tended to result in a new echelon of officials, who nevertheless lack the training which is given to Local Court magistrates. Village Courts are not supposed to handle problems arising from traffic accidents or tribal fighting. This in itself limits their potential contribution to the containment of violence at local levels. (4) Provincial Governments, with their policy secretariats and elected politicians vie with the national government and politicians for legitimate control of decision-making within their provinces. The kiap service comes under the responsibility of the Provincial Government of the Western Highlands Province. (See Appendices 1 and 2 for more detailed discussions of Village Courts, and the early stages of the Western Highlands Provincial Government's history.)

It is evident that several separate structures have been established, with none dominant to the extent that the kiaps were dominant in the eyes of the local people before self-government in 1973. Further, the activities of persons in these structures may in theory be separate and yet co-ordinated, but there is no integrated form of communication between them. It is only when areas are actually declared 'fight zones' that there are special arrangements for seeing that police and provincial officials do co-operate, for example. What is needed is co-operation *before* it becomes advisable to declare such fighting zones. Again, there is no single representative of the government at local level. Instead there are many, each belonging to a different arm of government. Too many government agencies can therefore lead in practice to too little government. There is no doubt, therefore, that in this sense administrative change did contribute to a 'breakdown in law and order' in the Highlands. But how exactly did it contribute? Not, I think, as a prime cause. Rather, we must see it as an enabling condition. Given other strains and tensions which were already developing, the communication hiatus or 'administrative gap' has allowed inter-group fights to grow and perpetuate themselves. As soon as one unsolved issue or one unavenged death has registered itself on people's consciousness, the ground is laid for chronic hostilities. Compensations and peace ceremonies may be held, but they are unlikely to end hostilities permanently. This does not mean that compensation is pointless; it is the only way to achieve at least an alternation of violent action with peaceful coexistence (see A. J. Strathern in Scaglion 1981).

Why did the administrative changes take place? For one thing, administrative problems were becoming more complicated, and the kiap system itself could not handle all of them. For another, the colonialist presumptions on which kiaps' activities tended to be premised had no true place in a nation which was to be independent. With the dismantling of the kiaps' powers their special sub-cultures also crumbled, partly because many of its 'carriers' left, partly because the sub-culture depended directly on the fact of effective power. The problem which emerged in turn from this, however, was that there was a need to develop a new ideology of field service, to make officers wish to go out on patrol and service rural areas, feeding the knowledge so gained into the structures of decision-making above them. It cannot be said that such a new ideology has emerged. Extension services are performed, but with better roads and transport, officials tend to visit briefly and return immediately to their town houses. The life-styles and culture which have carried over are those of the public servant, not that of the patrol officer, and local people in rural areas are unlikely to identify with such visiting officials or to accord them genuine friendship and respect unless they spend time actually living and talking with them. Exactly the same is true of politicians. As a Kawelka leader, Ndamba, put it to me when I spoke to him in April 1982 about a young aspirant who was challenging the sitting member in Dei Council: 'It is fine for you to mention his name and tell us that he is highly-educated. But if he wants our votes he must come here, show his face, and tell us what his ideas are. I do not even know what he looks like.'[3] Deep cultural assumptions underlie these remarks, and they are in contradiction with some of the values of bureaucracy. The bureaucrat is supposed to be 'faceless', whereas to Ndamba 'face', or personality, is vital. In the same way, when enemies fight, they no longer 'see one another's faces', but blacken their faces with charcoal to make themselves anonymous. When they wish to 'see the faces again', they make peace.

Notes

1 Mr Yanepa stood for election as a National Party candidate, this being a party which advocates capitalist development and a strong 'law and order' approach to government. He lost to the sitting member, Mr Barry Holloway, of the Pangu Party, which subsequently formed the new government.

2 Reverend Harland Kerr was based at Borona village about two hours' walk from Pangia station. He later established a new religious sect, although this was contrary to the Summer Institute of Linguistics' general policy.

3 The aspirant, Dokta-Mel, did not poll well in the election, for this reason. He polled 518 votes against the sitting member Parua-Kuri's 2,883.

3 Missions

The question of mission influence in Highlands societies poses very sharply the problem of the interaction between culture and social processes, for the reason that missions always deliberately set out to alter and replace the people's own culture, in both material and spiritual terms (see Robbins 1980 on the Southern Highlands Province). By contrast, the Australian Administration officers maintained a more complex attitude towards local practices. In respect of social structure, they tended to be 'conservationists': this structure must not be broken down, they reasoned, because if so, they would lose the reliable intermediaries between themselves and the mass of the people. Older 'fight leaders' were preferred by young kiaps, to 'junior upstarts' and 'bigheads' who might not listen to what the kiaps themselves said. If the Administration agreed with missions on any issue it was quite likely to be on different grounds from those used by the missionaries. For example, skull houses dedicated to dead kinsfolk in Pangia were removed by kiaps on the grounds that they were, in the early stages, an unhealthy attraction to bluebottle flies. The missions, however, wanted them banned as signs of devil-worship.

The point I wish to argue in this chapter is that the extreme dominance of missions in Pangia has led to a ritual attitude towards problems of change in the society. It is not simply a matter of the people adopting outward forms without appreciation of their supposed inner sense (Clark, in preparation 1982). Rather, it is that religion and other introduced practices are seen as *requirements* of progress. Pangia people quite understand that the missions preach of people changing their hearts and minds, not just their external actions. They are supposed to *tanim bel* (*tepe pekakoa meko*), a metaphor for leaving behind all the bad and evil things of the past, described as dirt, *ambe*, so that they can be washed clean by conversion to Christianity. The language by which the missions themselves approach conversion forces it into the realm of metaphor, and this is quite easily acceptable to the people, but such metaphor must be re-translated into action in order to be effective, they think. Hence ritual action and ritual attitudes.

Difficult questions of analysis arise here. It is my impression that Pangia people, as a result of intensive mission activity over the last twenty years, take Christianity rather seriously. By 'seriously' I mean that they regard its pronouncements as an important form of truth, especially in the twin dogmas of heaven and hell. This does not mean, however, that they are thereby able to discard entirely indigenous ideas about life and death. Indeed, the influence of the fundamentalist missions, at least, is such as to encourage a kind of continuing belief in indigenous spirit categories. These are necessary as 'devils' or 'Satans' against which the Christian has to fight in order to achieve entry into the Kingdom of God. They remain as real as ever, but are now designated as wholly bad, hostile, and dangerous, whereas God is good, loving, and beneficent. The freedom which the new doctrine brings, then, is certainly not the freedom of rational thought, but simply the freedom of having access to a superior power who can conquer the 'devils' of the past. But this also entails the possibility of doubt regarding power: what if God is not all-powerful? Moreover, spirit beings are tricky; they may be vanquished in one form only to reappear in another. One cannot be sure that they have died and will remain dead. Christianity, also, with its idea of the resurrection of Jesus, may itself support such attitudes. Furthermore, it has generated a genre of stories about men and women who have died and then returned to life, bearing stories of what Paradise looks like. If it is arguable that such people combine a tendency to epilepsy with a touch of the dramatic, to Pangia listeners, their statements are evidence of reality.

These considerations are introduced in order to indicate that there are good reasons why 'conversion' does not involve a wholesale re-thinking of the conceptual world by those converted. Rather, their world is deliberately incorporated, but marked with a negative sign, to stand against the positive one of the new religion. It is not that people lack an idea of logical consistency; it is simply that the way the new religion is communicated to them induces them to retain certain previous 'beliefs'. This may appear paradoxical, since overtly they are told to throw out their old beliefs and ways and to 'turn their stomachs'. At a deeper level, though, the paradox disappears: old beliefs are not treated as erroneous in a factual sense, but as morally wrong and dangerous. This explains why all aspects of ideas about mystical attack remain an essential part of the Wiru world view: these are attacks by ghosts, by a water-spirit whose name should not be spoken lest he come (*Uelali*, the 'water man'),[1] by the stick insect *kauwa*, by a kind of *sangguma* sorcery (*uro* or *maua*), by *nakenea* sorcery, by *tomo* sorcery, and by *kawei* spirits kept by a particular kind of ritual expert. Helpful, protective, or beneficent action is ascribed only to God. This point also helps to explain why the Wiru in fact suffer from considerable fear and suspicion that such attacks have been made on them: a quasi-paranoid ethos has been encouraged by this splitting of the religious perception of the world.

It is probable that the production of fear among the people has been a common effect of mission activities in the Southern Highlands. In at least two other places, Mendi and Tambul, the people have abandoned religious cults inherited from the past by burying cult stones in their cult sites, not because they no longer consider these objects have power, but simply in order to contain it. If they were to re-enter the sites and disturb the stones, their spirit power would be re-activated and large sacrifices would have to be made in order to propitiate them. If the stones are not to be disturbed, then neither should the knowledge of the cult be passed on, as such knowledge is for use in performance of the ritual. For this reason, old men refused to pass on cult details to a young national research worker of their own home area, even though he explained that he wished to collect this information in order to preserve it for posterity. 'Better that it should die with the cult rituals them-selves' the elders told him. Their attitude was rational enough, given the assumption that knowledge is power, and their wish to insulate future generations from exposure to the dangerous aspects of such power (Boyope Didi 1982). Close to Mendi town, a single prominent traditional leader who was also an MP, Mr Posu-Angk, up to 1982 maintained a set of cult houses in repair inside a ritual enclosure. He would handle the sacred stones and show them to selected visitors, such as myself, but others were far too afraid even to look at them properly. The round black stones that Posu kept up until he died in a car accident in 1982, were very heavy, and this was interpreted as a sign that they were full of spirit power.[2]

Such stones are known in Pangia as *tapa mu*, 'the testicles of the *tapa* spirit'. When missionaries entered the Pangia area, they tended to bring with them evangelists from neighbouring areas previously mission-ized. The Lutheran mission set up a station at Tiripini in 1960, the same year as Pangia Government Station was opened. The missionary, the Reverend William Hertle, initially made patrols by himself. Later evangelists from Hagen and Ialibu, to the north, settled into many of the newly-consolidated Wiru villages. They had small churches and schools built, and the evangelists called for children to attend their classes.[3] (It was a standing joke in Tunda that they tended to prefer young girls and used to tell them to 'place their lessons firmly into their stomachs'. A few evangelists left when their charges became pregnant.[7]) After a while they prevailed on the local people to build them houses, to make vegetable gardens for them, and to perform other daily tasks on their behalf. This was no doubt meant to supplement the tiny cash income they received from the mission, and to boost their status within their adopted communities, a status which was partly gained by their dramatic 'cult-breaking' patrols in the early 1960s. To show their superiority over the local cults they deliberately violated taboos on casual entry into sacred sites. They went further, taking out the *tapa mu* and throwing them away, even piling faeces on top of them. As people from Hagen, they doubtless could compare the Pangia cults directly with their own, and thus would know quite accurately how to defile them and so 'rob' them of their supposed power. For if the spirits did not punish them with sickness, this could only mean that the Christian God was protecting them and hence should be followed in preference to the traditional spirit entities.

The logic was irresistible, especially as it mimicked the demon-strations of strength employed by the kiaps. At the same time, the very rapid changes in custom which were forced upon the Wiru did produce a familiar kind of identity crisis, which expressed itself in an extended bout of 'madness' sweeping through all the villages in about 1961 (A. J. Strathern 1977a). By 1967, when I first did fieldwork at Tunda village, pre-1960 custom already seemed very far away; somehow the 'madness' marked a break with it. At the same time, a young man in his early twenties with whom I worked,[4] expressed bitter annoyance that the Lutheran mission had taken away all the fine things they had possessed before: cult practices, ways of honouring their dead, and forms of decoration.

Closer to Pangia station, the actions of some missionaries were, if anything, even more extreme. The Evangelical Bible Mission (EBM) insisted that all objects associated with pagan cults should be destroyed, especially the impressive painted wickerwork figures worn by dancers in the *timbu* cult. Such figures in fact might be allowed to rot traditionally after a cult performance, but the missionaries ordered them to be burnt forthwith and forbade their re-manufacture. Banning objects in this way was an effective way of apparently stamping out pagan religion, for the crucial knowledge that was tied up with such objects would eventually be lost, as in the case of the cult stones mentioned above. Ideas, however, can continue to be held without material realization, and until all the knowledge is lost, revival is always possible. On one or two occasions in Tunda, the revival of *timbu* has been mooted or rumoured, but it has never yet come about. The traumas of the 1960s still divide the people from their cultural past.

Spiritual warfare was not the only technique used by the missionaries. Jeffrey Clark has pointed out that in Takuru village, where he worked during 1981–82, the Wesleyan mission early on established themselves as purveyors of important material benefits (Clark 1982). By virtue of the village's isolation and the supply lines which they set up, they in fact justified this claim, but at the expense of being regarded in a material light by the people. Their 'success' story is one typical for the Highlands as a whole. They brought in a particular ideology, but were accepted for their practices rather than this, preserving dominance also by prescribing the cultural patterns which the people should follow in dress, hygiene, sexual practices – in short, their whole way of life.[5] The people adopted this new life-style out of a feeling of compulsion and obligation, but it also remains dependent on material exchange.

The Catholic mission, too, places a fair amount of emphasis on material transactions, but their overall handling of this is distinctive. They demonstrate skills by themselves building good churches, schools, and houses on their mission stations, and by setting up sawmills and health services on out-stations. In this way they make themselves indispensable. Moreover, they are in practice more tolerant of the outward manifestations of local culture than are the other missions. They encourage the wearing of traditional items of dress in church, for example. Catholic Fathers of the Capuchin mission, at Yaraparoi, close to Pangia Station, told me in 1967 that they had never directly told the people to do away with cult objects, and that these decisions were always those of the locals themselves. While such a claim must be regarded with some scepticism, it is a fact that in Pangia the Catholics have tended not to employ outsiders as evangelists, and from early on have trained villagers themselves to act as evangelists at their school in Erave, south of Pangia. These have now all returned and are based mostly in their own villages.

Between 1973 and 1975 (the period of self-government prior to the full Independence of Papua New Guinea) both of the major missions held major drives for baptisms throughout Pangia. No doubt several factors prompted them to do this. Many European missionaries were due to leave, and perhaps wished to do so with a sense of achievement. Local and imported evangelists were anxious to consolidate their positions of influence. Independence was to be a 'new time', so why not mark it with conversion to a new religion? Almost all the people had in any case been attending church and learning songs and responses by rote for many years. Baptism would also enhance the power of church elders to control the lives of those thus formally admitted to the body of the church, able to partake of its sacraments. No village held out, and scarcely any individual demurred. But the aftermath was not at all as the missions intended, for instead of a final break with pre-1960 culture, the event seems to have registered in the people's mind as an act giving them more liberty to choose for themselves which cultural practices were to be permitted and which not, just as in general Independence loosened the grip on them previously held by the kiaps.

Even so, no traditional cult revival took place. What did happen was that in one village, close to Tunda, in 1978–80, a leader took the initiative in constructing a type of longhouse, known as *Dapanda*, for which special rituals were appropriate. This was a political act in three senses. First, it was a statement of independence *vis-à-vis* the Lutheran mission. Now that national Independence had come, they should also follow the ways of custom and not be afraid to build such a house. Second, the leader, Kandi-Walipe, had recently been ousted from office by a rival, who had taken over the position of Local Government Councillor in Mamuane village. His decision to build the house was an indirect challenge to the new councillor regarding the control of labour in the village, since Kandi regularly needed men as 'carpenters' for his project.[7] Third, the house, once constructed, was also a challenge to the surrounding villages, particularly to the enemies of Mamuane, to build a house of equal beauty and strength. The types of timber employed for it all carried 'non-verbal' political messages to Mamuane's neighbours. For example, part of the wall was made with bark from the *okoi* tree, which was collected near Pupi and Maupini villages. These two villages were allies of Tunda in warfare against Mamuane, and recently the Pupi people had given pork to Leripini men, allies to Mamuane, followed by the death of one of the recipients. Taking the *okoi* bark and incorporating it into their own men's house was a challenge to the Pupi men. *Waluma* wood used stood for *Waluperi* one of the Peri groups at Tunda; *Pangio* for the village Tarini, within the Peri complex, since there is a Pangio tree standing there; *Andaiya* stood for 'old Tunda' where an Andaiya tree is to be found, and so on. The effect of all this was that the house actually consisted of a composite of symbolic equivalents or part-equivalents of the enemy groups around. It was thus a form of appropriation of the strength of those groups, a statement that the Mamuane men could control them, tantamount to a claim that they were already dead, since the strong trees which represented them were fastened into place on Mamuane ground. The Tunda men knew the names of the trees that had been used, for they had taken the trouble to inspect the house when it was under construction, on the pretext of visiting for some other purpose. In his speech at the pig kill for which the house was ostensibly constructed, Kandi emphasized strongly that he did not really mean any hostile intent by building the house, but rather it was made to keep the pearl shells given to Mamuane men; he enumerated by village where these shells had come from. Here he was stressing exchange ties through women, since pearl shells are given by wife-takers to wife-givers, who return cooked pork rib-cages at the time of pig killings. Tunda men do marry Mamuane women and vice versa; marriage does not follow the lines of military alliance (A. J. Strathern 1978).[8]

Kandi's house was something of a coup, both for himself as a leader and for the revival of custom in the Wiru area. The sequel, however, was not so happy. A combination of malaria and pneumonia hit his village after the pig kill (it is quite likely that the epidemic was brought by some of the visitors to the festival itself), and several men died. The mission supporters interpreted this as a kind of punishment from God, since the longhouse had been built on a traditional site and Kandi had disturbed the ashes from old fires lit by the men of yore. Their un-appeased ghosts, reminded of scores not settled with the enemies, had now sent this sickness to their own descendants, and God had declined to protect these because they had again taken up pagan ways. Kandi himself was not struck down, but some of his close kinsmen were, and the experiment in cultural revival was discouraged. There is no doubt that people were predisposed to see the sickness in Mamuane in these terms because of the cognitive structures set up by missions at an early stage of contact: that pagan spirits are dangerous and should not be tampered with.

There is also no doubt that a revival of custom at times of pig killings did also imply a revival of political hostilities between groups. Perhaps this helps to explain why this aspect of exchange was not very evident at the festival which I observed in 1967, when mission influence was at its height. *Kange* presentations, for example, which contain an element of prestige-seeking by big-men, were in abeyance at this time, yet flourish-ing again by 1978–80. Mission workers had no compunction about interfering with the progress of these festivals by insisting that the people all prayed together before they slaughtered the pigs; they also demanded that hymns be sung, and opposed the forms of self-decoration traditionally practised. For instance, one target was the elaborate bustle of different cordyline leaves used as a rear covering and carrying mess-ages to exchange partners and spectators. They also seem to have stopped women and girls, in particular, from decorating. The Hagen evangelists, who must surely have known that in their home areas no pastor would dare interrupt an exchange ceremony in such a way, roundly declared that they would see to it that no-one attempted to do anything 'pagan' with pearl shells. As late as 1980, in a village long influenced by the Evangelical Bible Mission, 'revivalists' held up the presentation of pork to visitors at a pig kill by conducting a hymn and prayer session first. On that occasion, however, it was noticeable that the recipients were fully decorated, and that they immediately got on with their own business after politely standing still during the imposed 'service'.

Another area of behaviour in which missions have attempted to exert a strong influence is family life. The main aim seems explicitly one of acculturation; family life must approximate the European Christian pattern. This is, of course, not a particularly easy aim to achieve, nor does it make a great deal of cultural sense. Marriage is an important part of the symbolism of the Christian churches, both being seen as the 'cornerstone of society' and as providing a metaphor for the relationship between Christ and the church. Hence every mission attempts to modify, if not abolish, traditional attitudes and practices in this sphere. The first and most obvious practice is polygamy. Since this is forbidden by Christian law, the missions simply refuse to give communion to anyone who remains party to a polygamous marriage. Polygamy is not so marked in Pangia as it is in Hagen, and Pangia women remark with bemused annoyance on the willingness of youngish Hagen women to become the third wives of older men, even when it is obvious that their husbands will die long before them. Nevertheless, cultural value is placed on polygamy by the big-men (*kamoango*) who therefore faced a dilemma when the baptism drive of the mid-1970s took place. Many big-men did not wish on the one hand to be left out of this drive, in case it might bring them advantage, or on the other to give up their plural marriages.

As it happened, on this occasion it was from the Christian side that an innovation was attempted. Dr Harland Kerr, a Summer Institute of Linguistics (SIL) fieldworker, who had lived in a Wiru village since very soon after the government Station had been opened, founded a sect which sought to give baptism to such men and their families. The Lutheran missionary opposed this strongly, and Kerr's move had no real official church status, since the SIL as such is not a church. But it was welcomed eagerly by the big-men, and in Tunda it was taken up by one with three wives and twenty children (Kumbea of Mandaiyawane Settlement). He built a little church for 'Harlo's' men to come and preach in. At this time, the Hagen evangelists and pastors had all gone back to the Western Highlands, since their work was declared at an end when the people were baptized and a local successor had been trained. The way was more open, therefore, for new sects to enter in this fashion. Later again, a new sect came to Kumbea's place: the Sios Bilong Kraist, a highly evangelistic American-based group, with head-quarters in Lae. A young Mandaiyawane man had worked for this mission in Lae and Mt Hagen and now brought them back to his home. They built a house for their own church teacher and a new church, after at first using the one set up for 'Harlo's' sect. The Lutherans sent their own man to contend with the new one, for the latter had no compunc-tion about open conflict with the established Lutheran pastor or about telling everyone that only his church properly understood the meaning of the Biblical texts. The leader's small settlement became a battle-ground for these minor sects, each seeming to differentiate itself from the established churches, much as the leader himself was differentiating his faction from the larger political blocs in the Tunda complex. He accepted these visitants partly because the young man of his lineage brought them, partly in hope of minor material reward, and partly because their presence lent a form of identity to his new settlement. Also, his eyesight was failing, and he attributed this to some unwitting act of sharing food with people who had killed a co-lineage kinsman of his by sorcery. The dead man's ghost had sent him this affliction because he had failed to 'see' his enemies in the first place. He was therefore worried about the future and the prospect of his death. Junior kinsmen at the same time determined to make a *kange* payment for him to his mother's people, saying that this would not be repeated after his death. Apparently this sect also did not object to his polygamy, for he and his family were re-baptized into it, thus making their third round of such 'conversions'. Possibly this was simply seen in an additive fashion, three times being better than once although that is scarcely the official policy of any mission.

Lutheran pastors and elders tended to toe a strict line on marriage and divorce, and this brought them into potential divergence with the practice of the kiaps. The patriarchal side of Christianity showed in decisions by pastors that couples should stay married, even if they were clearly unhappy and had not yet been baptized together. Since in almost all cases girls and women were the ones who objected to their marriages, it is clear that the dogma of the 'sanctity of marriage' worked to restrict women's freedom rather than that of men. Men were quite likely simply to set up a liaison with another woman and, when challenged, offer to marry her too and let the co-wives fight it out if they wished; otherwise one could leave him.[10] Of course, if the husband had been baptized, church elders would criticize him for this, but their only sanction was to refuse him communion. Heavy social pressure, by contrast, was brought to bear on girls, and since quite often their marriages had been arranged for them, it was more likely that they would attempt to escape from them and have to be coerced back. Suicide and threatened suicide sometimes resulted. Wiru sexual attitudes bear some similarities to those of the mid-Wahgi Kuma people in the 1950s described by Marie Reay: pre-marital freedom is followed by coercion and jealousy within marriage (Reay 1959). Moreover, in the Wiru villages several intermarrying groups are found together, a girl's previous sexual partners remaining nearby when she marries. Many girls continue with their liaisons, and a few men and girls are notorious as persistent 'philanderers' whose aim is to copulate with as many accessible partners in the village as possible. Overtones of incest often enter such relationships. These activities naturally upset the balance of numerous marriages, and one can understand the missions' viewpoint in wishing to make the Wiru more 'puritan' and to stabilize marriage as an institution. The analytical point, however, is that this desire was carried over from Christian cosmology and the Lutheran version of family life and sexuality, its roots therefore being entirely 'cultural' with the question of social welfare being secondary. Wiru church elders took up their policies for exactly the same reasons as their counterparts adopted the kiaps' word as law in administration: because it gave them power and because it shored up male control over females which was otherwise becoming somewhat weakened by the processes of social change that were occurring. Girls were instructed by their kinsfolk on how to present their cases to these mission headmen when the kinsfolk themselves wanted to break their marriage and switch partners. The actual dissolution of a marriage was made as hard as possible by the mission, and there would be protracted shuffling of the parties back and forth between the kiaps and the missionaries until a decision was reached.[11]

One of the interesting features of post-contact history in Pangia is the fact that up to 1983 there has been no activity comparable with the Hagen pearl shell cult of the 1940s and the money cult of the 1960s. There are two reasons for this. The first is that the supply of valuables never altered as dramatically in Pangia as it did in Hagen. Second, the Wiru experienced a concentrated push for cultural and social change that was thrust on them over two decades. They responded by obediently throwing away cult paraphernalia and practices, and by working hard at government projects such as road-building and maintenance. Their whole attitude to change was itself ritualistic, as if by total involvement in patterns of work they would achieve desired results. And this of course was what government officers endorsed, since wealth could only come through 'hard work'. It was by this combination of negative abandonment of traditional rituals and positive enthusiasm for government projects that the Wiru hoped the white man's power would come to them. They had to become 'like the white men', and that meant they should *replace* their previous practices with those appropriate to such an aim. In other words, they did not develop the more syncretic and multi-layered approach to social change that characterized the Hagen response to colonial intrusion.

The reasons for this difference between the two areas are not easy to discern, but generally they lie in a particular combination of historical and cultural factors. In historical terms, the impact of the European outsiders on Pangia was 'total'. In the space of a few years, fundamental efforts to transform the society were set in hand by the Administration, and the small numbers of Europeans with whom Wiru people came into contact all projected essentially the same image. Further, the Wiru, like other Highlanders, tend to attribute supernatural power to individuals who display unusual capacities, and Europeans were interpreted in this way. Clearly, therefore, the problem was how to become 'like them'. The same might be expected in the case of Hagen, but the emphasis is rather different. There, the chief cultural aim is to acquire and exchange products, and the new cults which Hageners invented in the 1940s were designed explicitly to meet historical crises in the supply of such wealth items, and connected with their perceived sources. The Pangia area has never experienced a sharp alteration in the supply of shells or money, nor is the demand for wealth as 'inflationary' as it is in Hagen, where the *moka* exchange system itself tends to boost demand. In the terminology which has been developed by Marilyn Strathern, the Wiru tend towards a metaphorical construction of wealth, whereas the Hageners tend to see it metonymically, a formula which fits the description given here. The metonymic construction goes with an aim of increase, whereas in the metaphorical construction, once the person has been substituted by the transfer of wealth, the symbolic purpose has been achieved (M. Strathern 1982).

None of the above is intended to deny that the influence of the missions on Hagen society has also been significant for social change in general. The Catholic and Lutheran missions have been established there since the 1930s, when their pioneers moved in on the heels of the government itself. Each set up a station just out of what is now Hagen township (Rebiamul was established by the Catholics, and Ogelbeng by the Lutherans) (see Vicedom and Tischner 1943–48; Mennis 1982). From these, evangelists gradually went out, teaching people hymns and telling them to build churches. Indeed, these activities were given a cargo-like twist by Hageners, who saw them as evidence of a new cult whose chants should be learned to give them access to white men's goods; churches were cult-sites, and to this day the idea that money is to be found in Christian cemeteries is very persistent. Of course, for many people nowadays such notions are submerged under a more official understanding of the church's role. But during the 1950s and early

1960s in Dei Council in the northern Melpa area, such claims were widespread and prepared the way for a more definite cult in the late 1960s (A. J. Strathern 1979–80; Brandewie 1981: 177). The rituals adopted by Lutherans also in a sense fed into this process. For they forbade their followers to handle shells (were these somehow seen as more evil than pigs?), and told them to wear trousers and shirts, not to enter cult-sites of the Female Spirit, nor to decorate themselves unduly for *moka*. They also encouraged the coalescence of separate settlements into mission villages centring on the church, and within these the merging of men's and women's houses into composite family dwellings. This last injunction conflicted with male ideas of female pollution, and led to big-men asserting that Christians clearly had no regard for the proper care of their bodies, since contact with menstrual blood is held to spoil the skin. Every one of these new rules can be seen as a kind of reversal of custom and its replacement by an antithetical form. Since the Lutherans also showed that they were keen on the 'modernization' process, in which the people should turn to cash, it was not unreasonably thought that the new taboos and practices were to contribute towards ensuring that access to cash was achieved.

Christian dogma is itself imbued with the idea of reversals and the triumph of the poor and weak over the rich and strong. Perhaps this is why successful big-men tend to remain pagan. Were they to be baptized, they could not keep their wives, decorations, shells – all the things giving them prestige. In 1964 one big-man (Ndamba) explicitly held a meeting in response to a request from the Reverend R. Jamieson, the missionary in his area, that he provide new candidates for baptism. The question he asked was, 'What rubbish-men have we got whom we can offer?' For the rubbish-men, too, perhaps baptism was seen as a means of improving their status, since they had little to lose by leaving the traditional system.

In certain respects, then, people in both Hagen and Pangia concurred in seeing the missions as bringers of benefits, the material side of things. Jeffrey Clark has noted that the Takuru mission in effect persuaded people to join it by virtue of its commanding position as a supplier of western goods. The Catholics in Pangia set up a health centre in Wiliame village, an unhealthy place far from the government Station, where malaria is prevalent. This clinic offers a better service than the Government Aid Post orderlies can offer. In Hagen, at Dei Council, when the Lutheran mission founded a station at Kotna in 1953, it set up a hospital and thereafter a mission-owned coffee plantation, which it subsequently transferred to the indigenous congregation. The Lutherans also founded the NAMASU marketing organization, which still runs the biggest store on the Pangia Station, and buys coffee throughout the Highlands. The Seventh Day Adventists shores up its policy of forbidding the consumption of pork by encouraging its adherents to start cattle projects and so replace illicit pork with beef. This mission kept a small outpost, manned by a couple from North Solomons Province, just outside Tunda village in the late 1960s, and the evangelist visited Tunda on Saturdays to show pictures of heaven and hell along with a tin of corned beef which he advised people to eat if they wished to go to the right place after death. The Adventists, however, suffered from the disadvantage of not having a main station in Pangia itself. They had sent an evangelist early in the 1960s to Kundu village a few miles from Tunda, and this man attracted several girls from neighbouring villages to his 'school', using his position to seduce them. The girls went to him in the first place partly in defiance of their seniors and the already established Lutheran mission. But, as one of them recalls, when they smelled the odour of cooking pork and were not invited to share in such feasts by their fathers, they came back home. Quite commonly, girls have married into one mission, and subsequently changed their affiliation by re-baptism into a new church when they marry a new husband, a kind of 'baptismal polyandry'. Almost all the Hagen evangelists have returned home to the Western Highlands, and Pangia people who have seen them there realize that they are of no particular status in Hagen itself, their status in Pangia depending entirely on mission colonialism. In return for the 'knowledge' they gave and in respect for the power which was assumed to go with it, the people gave these evangelists free labour, built their houses and churches, made their gardens, and carried their stores from the station. Pangia people in the 1960s had very little access to cash except for what was brought in by returning contract labourers, and it had never been their practice to build houses for their big men or to make gardens for them without material reward. The evangelists' tiny cash income and ability to command services with the backing of the white missionaries was therefore impressive. By the mid-1970s, however, the situation had changed; cash income had gradually risen, and the evangelists were departing. Consequently, perceptions changed. Pangia people found themselves regarding these men as 'rubbish' rather than as big-men or even 'white men' (*kianango*) as they had done only ten years before. Historical and material circumstances thus determined how the mission's agents were seen.

The destruction of overt customary practices in Pangia, and their erosion and attrition over time in Hagen, have been accompanied by a corresponding adoption of mission and western-inspired custom. Most recently, the missions themselves have attempted to incorporate more elements of indigenous custom into their own rituals, in a bid to come to terms with the facts of political Independence. The Catholics early on encouraged traditional dress, and the Lutherans stage displays of decorated dancers at times of baptism. There is a standard melodrama which they enact, in which the followers of Satan are represented as evil warriors from the past, their bodies blackened with soot and rubbed in mud, twanging arrows at the white-robed initiands. The dominant images still propose that what is traditional is evil, except that a place is also found for legitimate self-decoration by relatives of those to be baptized. One mission which has made no steps in this direction is the Evangelical Bible Mission, for which all manifestations of traditional culture are intrinsically wrong. It was this mission which in the early 1960s was responsible for people 'speaking in tongues' at their conversion and for burning sacred objects. In 1967 a party of its workers, together with their missionary leader, passed through Tunda village on their way back from a patrol to Pulupari where they were setting up a new station. As it happened, two boys were walking up to my house at precisely the same moment wearing on their heads a pair of wickerwork representations known as *timbu wara* and previously worn at the final stages of the *timbu* cult; I had commissioned these to be manufactured as examples for an artefact collection. I greeted the missionary and asked him in for a cup of tea, should he be so inclined. Over my shoulder he and his carriers saw the *timbu wara*. The men muttered 'Satan, Satan' in shocked disbelief, and the missionary turned, a little abruptly, and bade me good-day. He had already been personally responsible for burning these objects, whereas the Catholics merely bought them to decorate their houses. Later, after 1975, this same man broke away from the Evangelical Bible Mission based at Mele village in order to found a truly indigenous church, much the same attempt as Harland Kerr. He went to Mamuane village near Tunda on the way to Pulupari, built a house and began discussing how such a church could be created. While he was away one day, a fire broke out in his house, and all his family's possessions were destroyed, along with the house itself. As it had been built on ground disputed between Tunda and Mamuane, there was some question as to how the fire had begun; in any case the missionary was forced to leave and return to the United States. It is interesting that he began his missionary career by burning sacred artefacts, and ended it when his own house was burnt. It is also interesting to note that in 1980 when the new evangelist mission, Sios Bilong Kraist, came to Tunda it began to do business by buying up the people's artefacts and decorations – another way of separating them from their culture. It is unclear to me what this mission does with the items purchased.

Details of the ways in which customs were eroded are sometimes hard to establish. For Pangia, no ethnography was written at the time of contact itself. By 1967, vast surface changes had occurred. The person who knows most about the topic is Harland Kerr of the SIL, yet he has published little of his extensive research work. In Hagen, rich early ethnographies were written by the Lutheran missionaries, and these give a valuable baseline for discussion (Vicedom and Tischner 1943– 48). But the period in which decisive changes took place, at least in Dei Council, as it became in 1962, was about 1950–60, immediately after the mission station at Kotna was built. During this time, the progress of spirit cults into Dei from the Central Melpa was halted; indeed these were in abeyance at the time in their strongest traditional centre, the Nebilyer Valley. The second major effect of mission work was the removal of many of the overt signs of the cult of family ghosts, with which a large part of Melpa morality is bound up (M. Strathern 1968). The same happened in Pangia in the 1960s, but in a more extreme fashion, since sites there were actually desecrated by Hagen evangelists fresh from a decade of practice in the destruction of their own religion. All those containing skulls were dismantled and the remains reburied in cemeteries, along Christian lines.[12] In Hagen, small round houses, *kor manga rapa*, 'spirit men's house', were traditionally built to contain the skull of an immediate forebear, and in these small pigs were sacrificed by household heads when settlement members were sick or when they felt they needed the advice or support of the ghosts in any enterprise. In 1964 a few could still be seen in Dei, without the skulls; Ongka, for example, in a manner typical of big-men, still kept one. In Pangia, I did not see such a shrine until I crossed the border between Pangia and Erave Sub-district. At once I found a row of skulls in a box and another wrapped in bark and placed in the fork of a tree. Enquiring about these, I was told simply 'that the Erave kiap told us to retain these things in case we should have a use for them in future'. They knew that in Pangia it had been different, and all had been swept away. No doubt this was one reason why the EBM extended its attention to Pulupari in the 1970s.

Another practice which was unequivocally forbidden as devil-worship in Pangia was that of carrying the dried hands of dead relatives as neck decorations. This was a mark of remembrance for the hand which had held them and given them things (gift-giving is referred to as 'showing one's hand' to people, *yono yamereko*; receiving is to 'see the hand', *yono eneko*). A mother might also keep the bones of a deceased child hanging up in a netbag wrapped in sweet-smelling grass, until her next child is born.

While the apparent effect of these changes was to remove traditional religious practices and substitute for them Christian ones, the real situation in both areas was, and remains, much more complicated than this. In both places, for slightly different reasons, traditional healing rituals are still performed, and seem to have been maintained continuously, even while other major changes were occurring. And the ideas held about ghosts have never been fundamentally altered. Indeed in Pangia the evangelical missions, as I have noted, preserved the idea of ghosts as malevolent entities as a contrast with the Christian God. The water-spirit (*Uelali*), sangguma sorcerers (*maua*), and *kawei* spirits which act under the control of a ritual specialist, are all still held to exist, and the structural conditions under which these concepts flourished have scarcely altered. That is, the society is divided into loose territorial blocs associated with village names, and within these there are also multitudinous rivalries over land, sexual activities, pigs, crops, and valuables. Communication between blocs does not necessarily reduce tension. Indeed, it may facilitate the diffusion of techniques of, for example, sorcery. In the 1960s the dreaded *maua* technique was held to be practised only by fringe Wiru living nearest to the Erave area. Now, however, it is said to have spread almost throughout the language area, or at least as far as the Pangia Station. Ghosts also appear regularly in people's dreams in Pangia, coming to take people away on long journeys to the land of the dead. Their faces hidden, they rape and entice; they stuff faeces or putrifying brain matter into people's mouths, so that they wake feeling suffocated (this is called *tondoka mereho*, 'giving a sausage'). A woman's dead husband repeatedly returns to her to have sexual intercourse and take her away with him, and vice versa, an idea which motivates spouses to prevent one another's death. *Yomberono*, traditional bark and leaf medicines, are much valued as means of staving off the presence of such jealous dead sexual partners, and the *kuliali*, or experts, who keep them do good business.

In Hagen, the nexus of ideas in which the need for traditional-style ritual action is maintained is that of *popokl*, anger or frustration, and sickness. Indeed, it was precisely this nexus which drew the hostility of Lutheran and Baptist mission workers in the 1950s. *Moka* exchange, they claimed, leads to such *popokl*, and therefore to bad rather than good social relations, hence it must be forbidden, because the Christian must not have *popokl* in his or her heart. The argument was socially absurd, since *moka* does lead to on the whole good social relations, and the indigenous ideal itself is not to succumb to *popokl*, for the good reason that to do so invites ghosts to send sickness. While such sickness may be sent out of pity, if the person does not overcome the *popokl* which caused it, death may result. *Popokl* is removed by the sick person explaining the source of anger, on the one hand, and by the sacrifice of a pig on the other. The latter is required in order to make the ghosts release the soul or *min* of the patient, so that it can return to its body. Communication with the ghosts is maintained through the *noman* or 'mind' of the person, and therein lies the possibility of essential continuity even when external forms of action have been removed. Prayers, *kng atenga*, were previously spoken aloud by an expert or big-man at the moment when pigs were clubbed and their spirits thus separated from their bodies – they must be struck properly with the club so that they die quickly and their blood does not gush too freely from the nose. Through association with me, knowing my interest in such practices, Ndamba and Ongka, two Kawelka big-men, have both taken to speaking these prayers aloud again in recent years. The style is intense, deliberate, concentrated, like a quieter version of public oratory. But the point is that, even without such a revival, in essence sactifices continued without any historical break at all, since a person always thinks something in the *noman* at the time of killing a pig, and this thought automatically is communicated to the ghosts. Even if, again, a Christian prayer is pronounced instead, it is thought that the ghosts are present and are informed of the social situation.

Ritual action towards ghosts is often performed at night, at at least in privacy. If one does not know people well, one will never see it; one is shown it only if one has a long involvement with the people concerned. Thus, Wömndi of Kawelka Kundmbo clan took me along when in 1978 he finally threw out some relics of his father Kondi who had died in 1976. He cast these into some undergrowth near his father's old men's house, which Wömndi no longer uses. Kondi's spirit is held still to inhabit this area and had taken to bringing with it into the house a wild spirit (*tipu römi*) which also lived there, so Wömndi's act had the

character of an apotropaic ritual, telling Kondi to stay where he was outside. Wömndi performed the act of throwing out his father's relics (bark
belt and hair-wig) by himself and informed no-one other than myself
that he was doing so. In other cases, more men will be involved, as when
the soul of a man killed away from home is called back by his clansmen or
when a night divination is held to question a newly-dead man on the
cause of his demise. But all these acts are kept away from other clan kin,
and they are of the kind which can escape the notice of mission pastors.

In this chapter I have argued that the missions have mounted their
work of social change explicitly in terms of cultural change, in effect an
attack on traditional cultural forms. My other point has been that this
attack has emerged with rather different historical results in Hagen and
Pangia. In Pangia, mission influence has been intensive and dominant,
and has at the same time preserved a 'devalued' stereotype of indigenous ideas. The response of the people has been to 'obviate' their own
practices in order to take up those of the missions. But the obviation is
partial and reversible, and longer acquaintance with the area since 1967
confirms that the basic categories and ideas of the Wiru have not been
fully replaced. God functions rather as a protector against indigenous
spirits, and this in itself reinforces dependency feelings generated
during the colonial period, even when the Wiru are basically running
their own church affairs.

In Hagen, Christianity operates in a much less dominant manner.
Here too, indigenous ideas remain largely intact, preserved in a nexus
of ideas and practice; but in addition, because of the support they have
from a number of big men, indigenous practices retain more equality
with those appropriate to Christianity. An example of this is to be
found in the spatial juxtaposition of the Female Spirit cult-site in the
Kawelka Kundmbo territory with that of the Lutheran church, an
uneasy, segmentary tolerance holding between the two cult forms. The
difference between Hagen and Pangia, therefore, is not that in the
former area traditional ideas have persisted while in the latter they have
not. In both, the basic structure of traditional ideas remains strong.
The difference lies rather in terms of historical overlay, leading to
mission dominance in one case and a more balanced situation in the
other. Since 'history' is just as 'total' in its reference as is 'culture', this
proposition regarding the missions must be seen as merely a part of the
wider spectrum of change and continuity. I will proceed to other parts
of the spectrum; in the next chapter I consider administrative and
political history.

Notes

1 *Uelali* also corresponds in Wiru to the Daribi culture-hero character, Souw, otherwise known as Sido or Tiro (Wagner 1974).

2 Posu was almost a charismatic figure. His mantle fell upon his brother, William Mona Ank, who was elected in his place in the 1982 national election in Mendi open electorate. Before his death Posu had been planning to turn his cult site into a tourist attraction, but he would not allow photographs or notes to be taken inside the enclosure.

3 It was a standing joke in Tunda that they preferred girl pupils, whom they used to tell to 'place their lessons firmly into their stomachs'. A few evangelists left as a result of pregnancies. The same was said of the Seventh Day Adventist who set up a school at Kundu village not far from Tunda. The Tunda girls used to attend this school at least in part out of opposition to their fathers. They would refuse to attend church on Sundays, since their Sabbath was over on Saturday, and walked off up to the gardens by themselves, an action clearly of a provocative nature. One woman recounts how her father, to teach her a lesson, once cooked a pig and announced that as she was now a Seventh Day Adventist she would not be sharing in the meat. She had to endure the rich smell of pork and vegetables and watch the others eating the pieces her father gave them. Her frustration was the greater because it was a favourite practice of the children of a polygamist, as her father was, to compete vigorously for sweet pieces of meat so that they could claim his special favour for themselves and their part of the family. She gave up the Seventh Day faith at this time.

4 This was Kapu-Takuna, who acted as my assistant from 1967. His father had been a notable big man of the Epea group, associated with the Windiperi clan.

5 The Evangelical Bible Mission and Wesleyans also encourage trance-like behaviour in church. When the Holy Spirit comes to them, they tremble at the knees and call out *ke-ke ke-ke, Anutu*, a form of thanksgiving to God. Similar practices, 'speaking with tongues', are fostered by the new and very popular Pentecostal churches in the Southern Highlands and in Port Moresby.

6 One woman noted with surprise how easy it was by comparison to get baptized in the Lutheran church in Port Moresby, without previous lengthy classes or labour-service.

7 I first discovered the project when I attended a Village Court hearing at Mamuane. The Councillor was attempting to place in gaol several of the men who were working for Kandi – a typical piece of Wiru in-fighting. Kandi defended himself stoutly as a legitimate upholder of custom, and appealed to me to obtain National Cultural Council support for his longhouse building, a request which I complied with and successfully met.

8 The non-correspondence of marriage frequencies and political alliance means that even between several hostile villages important individual ties exist.

This contradiction seems to be reflected in an extreme ambivalence of social relations and an intense suspicion of 'veiled talk' and sorcery.

9 And in particular since big-men are the target for sorcery attacks and have usually instigated many such themselves during their careers they are afraid that at any time they may die and have to go to hell because they were not saved in time by baptism while alive.

10 What men do not like to do is explicitly to tell their wives that they no longer want them, because if they do so their claim to any return of bride-wealth is weakened. Inevitably, then, divorce always takes on the appearance of being initiated by the wife.

11 At an early stage of administration the first appointed *bosboi* ordered the punishment of women by mass copulation. The woman was forced to lie down and her arms and legs were tied to the ground before this occurred.

12 Certain customs to do with the fear of ghosts also came under mission attack. If a beautiful young girl died, her limbs were broken in the grave and her eyes closed up with deep red juice from the *kung* plant so that the ghost would not see its way to attack its living kin. It is assumed that those who die before their time are jealous of the living. It is also dangerous for a pregnant woman to be near a cemetery, for the 'coldness' of the place may affect the baby living inside her, and any ghost of a woman who died without giving birth is bound to attack her.

4 Kiaps, councillors, and politicians

Kiaps, both as agents of the Administration and as individuals, were enormously influential in the Highlands from the 1930s to the 1960s. Since 1970 their influence has been on the wane, and this correlates in time with the emergence of obvious social and political problems in the region as a whole. Kiaps and ex-kiaps have therefore sometimes argued that these problems have actually resulted from the dismantling of the system of patrolling set up by expatriate officers with generalist powers during the colonial period. From their own viewpoint, there is some truth in this. In fact the switch from a simple to a complex form of administration at local level has certainly led to a paradoxical 'administrative gap', for while there are more officials now directly concerned with this level, hardly any of them are ever to be seen actually visiting clan areas. But the answer to today's problems does not lie simply in bringing back the kiaps to do their patrolling act. Heraclitus's proposition holds: you cannot step into the same river twice.

I have already looked at the question of administrative and political change in a number of publications on Hagen (A. J. Strathern 1974, 1977b). This has largely been because the problems have presented themselves in a more obvious manner, and the argument on patrolling has been broached more definitely there since patrols declined in Hagen at an earlier date than in Pangia. What I have not done before is to examine contrasts between Hagen and Pangia at any length. The main contrast is in line with my observations so far. While in both areas there is inter-group conflict, in Hagen this is most noticeable at a high level between whole clans and/or tribes, while at lower levels there are stronger controls on disputes. In Pangia the reverse holds: large-scale fighting is practically unknown, but small-scale disputes are endemic, require constant attention, and cause continual strain within local communities. Concomitantly, in Hagen, while there is certainly rivalry over the position of Local Government Councillor at periodic elections, this is in no way as intense as it is in Pangia, even though objectively the structure of local government is the same for both areas. The positions of provincial and national politicians, however, are eagerly contested in both places, chiefly because of the definite material benefits which such office-bearers obtain. They are seen to represent also the wider polity and the world beyond the language area, and this makes their positions deeply attractive to those who wish to replace the old-style big-men with an equivalent 'modern' form. Younger educated men are therefore more and more entering this level of contest, while at the same time finding that to win they need to have or to acquire status in other spheres of activity. Efforts to short-cut the laborious processes whereby such status can be won are therefore to be expected, and these have to be made in the cultural idiom of exchange. By the time of the 1982 national elections this problem had become very evident, and led to many arguments over bribery and corruption.[1] Indeed, it is noticeable that such accusations tend to attach to the activities of almost any official role-holder in the introduced system of politics and administration, and this holds for both Hagen and Pangia, the reason being that the idea of such offices is still new and has no indigenous counterpart. The development of effective inbuilt controls on the conduct of such office-holders has, however, been slow. Along with the assumption of corruption and complaints against it, there also exists a kind of tolerance of it. Since office-holders may be, and often are, voted out, they have only a circumscribed period in which to make their mark and ensure that they are materially well off. Further, any wealth is needed when they next stand for election, since they will require it to in effect buy votes. This emerging indigenous pattern is in sharp contrast with the colonial ethic of public service and politics as the act of 'serving the

people', which the kiaps promulgated. Yet it has partly been 'produced' by the kiap era, during which the foundations were laid both
for the commercial exploitation of the Highlanders' resources and for
the ensuing social inequality, with its notion that power can be demon-
strated by arbitrary or 'despotic' behaviour. In practice the kiaps were
often seen by local people as arbitrary in their decisions, and it is this
image which has in part been inherited by the politicians.[2]

The first step in dismantling the kiaps' role came with the creation of
the Local Government Councils, in 1962 in Dei Council and 1965 in
Pangia, in both cases two years before my fieldwork began. This dismantling process was disguised at the outset by the fact that locally
resident expatriate patrol officers were appointed as advisers to the
councils. At the outset they dominated them, showing their superiority
by telling the councillors how to dress for meetings and how to speak in
turn or put and vote on motions. Councillors had to learn a whole new
uncomfortable repertoire, subject to the kiaps' paternalistic control; in
effect the kiaps were teaching a new sub-culture of leadership practices.
While they avoided any direct influence on who was elected to council-
lorships, kiaps also acted as executive officers for the holding of elections, and what they had to say was regarded as important by electors.[3]

The role of councillor in the 1960s was supposedly distinguished
from that of the *luluais* and *tultuls* who had preceded them in two
ways. First, the former agents had been a direct part of the kiaps' hierarchy, and it was part of their job to settle disputes. There are many
stories of how early *bosbois* and *tultuls* used the new colonial mystique
to terrify people and to extract large fines from alleged offenders
against the kiap's laws, of which they were the privileged transmitters.
Councillors, by contrast, were not given any court functions. Instead,
they had the new task of being development agents, of persuading and
organizing the people towards projects for economic and political
change. Councillors meeting together were supposed to develop a
political consciousness beyond that of their clan wards. In practice,
however, they interpreted their role as including, rather than excluding, the earlier *luluai*/ *tultul* role, and chafed under the knowledge that
the kiap expected them to transmit his orders to the people while denying them either his own powers or those of previous functionaries.

The above applies to Dei Council and summarizes my own earlier
observations. In Pangia at this time Council Advisers certainly behaved
in the same way as in Dei, but the people's response was conditioned by
their greater sudden encapsulation in the colonial system. Councillors

were afraid of the kiap, and at the same time used his pronouncements as a powerful means of backing up their own potentially rather weak position. They threw themselves with great apparent enthusiasm into road-building, house repairs, latrine construction and the like and were hard on minor offences. *Bosbois* were appointed with specific briefs to report on any slackers at community work and these were apprehended under Native Regulations. The kiap, of course, could at the time both arrest and try such offenders, and two months' gaol was the usual punishment. Councillors accepted that the kiap was the one who heard cases, but they used their position strongly to influence what cases came to the kiap's notice and how they were presented. It is likely that the sheer pressure on the kiaps of this litigation eventually encouraged them to pass this function on to Local Court magistrates, and subsequently to the Village Courts that were set up in 1979.

As has frequently been pointed out, the position of councillor *vis-à-vis* kiap was weak largely because the latter still held court powers. Kiaps could, and did, hear cases against councillors and place them in gaol for criminal offences, reducing effective co-operation. Patrol officers clearly felt in the early 1960s that councillors were often lazy, corrupt, and inefficient, and that they themselves could better put over the government's message to the people. Councillors did indeed have difficulty in reporting back fully on the business of meetings, as they were expected to do. They held Sunday meetings before or after church services in Tunda village, but these occasions were likely to turn into general discussions of court cases, usually involving sexual relationships, or plans for pig killings.

The two matters which recur endlessly in both areas in the discussions of the 1960s are roadworks and the payment of tax. In Dei the tax rate for men rose from $A2 to $A10 in the space of some five years, while in Pangia it remained at $2. With the sharp rise in Dei came a willingness to question the Council as a body bringing benefits to local communities. Councillors began to be seen as minor politicians whose role should be to secure an aid post, school, road extension, or development project for their ward constituency. These were based quite firmly on the existing clan structure in Dei, as determined by an initial kiap-run survey (carried out by Mr Max Allwood). Hence councillors had behind them social groups which also operated as such in local politics, outside the council system, and were therefore likely to ask their councillor to act as their representative in matters of material interest. In Pangia, the kin-based local groups tend to be smaller than Dei, and councillors normally represent villages with numerous small descent groups. They therefore have a less solid basis of support, and this makes it more likely that they will use their government status to impose decisions. They are also more likely to be challenged and opposed within their wards, even though they in theory have as their supporters *komiti* (Pidgin English) men appointed to secondary positions, who mostly come from group sections other than that of the councillors. This is also the case in Dei, but there the wards are more unitary, and although there are definitely internal oppositions within them, these are not as strong as in Pangia. There an election is usually held for the *komiti* positions as well as that of councillor; whereas in Dei the division of *komiti* badges is more often decided informally, the councillor himself having the greatest say as to who should possess them. This is both because of the ward structure as such and because competition for these positions is not as fierce as in Pangia.

Political dissent correspondingly emerged earlier in Dei, and has been very noticeable since 1975. Refusals to pay tax are common, not by outright disobedience, but usually by failing to turn up on tax day and making oneself difficult to find later. Wards which lack a strong councillor really do lose out on development projects, and people are increasingly aware of this. The Council's finance committee is very influential in deciding the disposition of funds, since its members hold a closed meeting prior to the main Council meeting and make decisions which they proceed to push through later, over the heads of less well-briefed and forceful councillors. In the elections of 1982 among the Kawelka, these points were strongly emphasized by Yap-Roklpa, a young partly-educated man who stood for office as a successor to Ongka, the outstanding leader who held the councillorship for all the Kawelka. Yap's small group, the Klammbo, are the least numerous among the Kawelka segments, yet he was able to win, partly because he had support in both of the main Kawelka settlement areas and partly because younger voters really did recognize the need for a shift away from traditional style big-man representation in the Council. Yap had formed an alliance with a cross-cousin of his mother's group, Goemba Kot, who is a prominent Dei businessman, and the latter had made him a director of one of his plantations. Yap was convinced that if he was elected, he would also become a member of the finance committee of the Council and so would bring his group more into the centre of Council-supported activities.[4]

Yet the Council obviously suffers from an overall shortage of funds for projects. The tax rate has remained static at K10 per head for men and K1 for women, yet costs have risen. A major source of extra revenue comes from a coffee plantation purchased by the Council with a large government loan in 1976 – Tigi plantation, founded by John Collins. Income from this is disposed of by the Council, mostly going on new road projects. In the past people paid their taxes out of fear of the kiap, much as they turned out for censuses, road-work and medical inspections, but now the Council executive officers and clerks, who do not have the power of a kiap, find it hard to persuade everyone to pay. The clerks themselves have from time to time been accused, even convicted, of embezzling Council monies, and this also does not encourage people to pay up. The level of interested democratic participation in Council matters has also declined since Independence. Previously there was mass attendance at the AGM in Dei, when the people were invited to decide for themselves what rate of tax they would pay in accordance with their aims for the coming year. The debates were lively, and Council officials by no means always had their way. But these AGM occasions no longer appear to be held. While the Council thus begins to be more remote from the people, its real functions are gradually being taken over by the new Provincial Government. Positions in the Provincial Assembly are becoming a more important power base than the officers of Council President and Vice-President, which were greatly coveted prior to 1975. Predictably, Council officers in turn complain that the Provincial Government fails to allocate funds for their area, or is operating corruptly.

In Pangia, interest in the Council system is still strong. All government agents, as well as the missions, continue to act as controllers of people's work patterns. The Lutheran mission, for example, makes its adherents do community service and attend baptismal classes for as long as two years before they can gain the benefit of full entry into the church. Councillors still command people to work on the roads, a pattern which has almost totally disappeared in Dei and was already on the wane in the late 1960s. In Dei also, people simply put down their names for baptism, and need not attend lengthy classes as a prerequisite of baptism. Interest in the Council is at its strongest at election time; these are held every three years. In Tunda village the office has ever since 1965 alternated between the two most powerful blocs, the same two individuals, Kelo and Koke, representing the Windiperi and the Waluperi-Leonoperi blocs respectively, maintaining their rivalry throughout the period. The Leonoperi have never contested the councillorship as such, being content always to retain a *komiti* position. Angaliri, theoretically the pair-group of Windiperi, have similarly refrained from putting up their own candidate and have instead always retained a *komiti*'s badge, but their allegiance to Windiperi in elections has been doubtful. Since Windiperi are much more numerous than Angaliri and tend to dominate them, the latter have attached themselves instead to Waluperi – or, rather, they have divided over this. One basis of their opposition to Windiperi is the long-standing rivalry between Kelo of Windiperi and the Angiliri big-man Kumbea. The split between these two was intensified in 1970 when Waima, an Angaliri man, died, and suspicion attached to the Windiperi as the probable agents of sorcery against him, along with two sub-groups of Kerepali village, Weka and Kapuri. Angered at this, the Angaliri gave their votes to Koke in the next election, and he won. Since then they have continued to hold the balance of voting power in the village. Kelo has profited from an internal quarrel between Kumbea and Kewa of Angaliri, securing the latter's allegiance to himself, and has also held some Angaliri through their affiliation to the Lutheran mission. Koke was, however, removed from office in 1978, after the Windiperi had expanded faster in population than his own group's Waluperi. Kelo turned the councillorship over to his younger brother Tamau, and rewarded Kewa with the *komiti* badge. Koke contested the correctness of the election, claiming that Tamau's narrow win had been occasioned by his importation of two extra voters from Pupi village, as well as by the unfortunate absence of a few of his crucial Angaliri supporters. He planned to take his objection as far as the new Provincial Secretary in Mendi, Roy Yaki. However, nothing much happened, and in the meantime Tamau distinguished himself by remaining silent at all meetings, since he had no command of Pidgin English and was unable therefore to talk with anyone other than Wiru speakers. Koke also secured for himself a position on the panel of Village Court magistrates, set up in 1978, and in 1980 was made the chairman of the panel centred on Windi Courthouse near Tunda. In 1982 he was re-elected back into his councillorship as well, while Kelo was appointed Land Mediator, a position once held briefly by Kumbea and vacated by him when he failed to settle a number of minor disputes, this kind of role not being his forte. Kelo was highly zealous in his new job, travelling widely, listening intently to disputes, and complaining sadly that his minuscule allowance was unduly slow in being forwarded through the national Justice Department. He was clearly determined to 'hold his end up' in the face of Koke's success as a powerful figure in the Village Court system.

By the time of the 1978 elections, the last expatriate kiaps had left Pangia Station, and with the introduction of the Provincial Government, district administration was revised, the role of Assistant District Commissioner being replaced by that of District Manager. The final vestiges of the kiap's authoritarian and almost chief-like position were thus removed. Up to mid-1977, however, lone kiaps posted to Pangia still made their one-man patrols. The last one completed a whole set of re-investigations into land disputes in 1977, recommending that many of them be heard by the Land Titles Commission and meanwhile re-affirming that such disputed land was to remain unused. He then left, and since then patrolling has simply ceased to exist. This disappearance has had two effects. One is that the pressure to perform community work is not quite as severe as it was before, and as a result the Pangia link road, never very safe or smooth, has become distinctly rough and dangerous in wet weather. Second, the officials whose positions were created to fill the gap left by the kiaps have variously assumed aspects of their sub-culture. There is little doubt that the most obvious transmission of this sub-culture has been in the sphere of hearing disputes in court. Village Court magistrates now approximate the role of the kiap.

It is in the capacity to settle disputes between persons that power is most readily seen, since those who disobey a court ruling can be fined or placed in gaol. Prior to pacification and kiap rule, dispute-settlement was weak in Pangia. This is not to say it did not happen, but the numbers and influence of big men were smaller than in Hagen. Stick fights, sorcery, and sometimes collective rape of recalcitrant women, were practices resorted to in order to control behaviour or to avenge losses. Councillors lost this power when the switch-over from *bosboi-tultul* system took place in 1955, and it re-surfaced only when the Village Courts were set up. The purpose of these, as envisaged by their legal planners in Port Moresby, was to restore customary powers to the local people. Yet where such power did not customarily exist, it is evident that this was an impossibility. To give themselves legitimacy, these courts had rather to inherit the mantle of the kiaps and of the itinerant Local Court magistrates who had replaced them. Rather than operating informally, as intended, then, Village Courts were marked by formality and ritual, so as to impress those who came before them with the weight of their presence. Koke, for instance, quickly learned how to use this new ritual, and made himself a house near the court area as well as often choosing to deliver his homilies in Pidgin rather than Wiru, his ideas and expression, however, being more subtle and humorous than those of the kiaps. Regardless of whether there is minor corruption associated with the taking of fine payments in these courts – and this is universally suspected – they are the nearest thing to filling the 'administrative gap' I mentioned earlier, and successful magistrates are beginning to consolidate themselves as the true possessors of power, in contrast with the councillors.

Politicians 'proper', of course, are the other possessors of such power, and this they are supposed to exercise in their assemblies at provincial and national levels. They do so, however, sporadically, and their actions are not regularly witnessed by local people, whereas those of the Village Court magistrates are. This court seems to have met an important local demand for places of litigation close to home, and it thus absorbs a great many of the minor tensions and quarrels that are so characteristic of community life in Pangia. The sub-culture of the kiaps blends here with the easy knowledge and wit of village savants, and together these make the institution effective. The 'success story' is less definite in Dei, and I shall now examine why this is so.

When the Council was set up in Dei, councillors were not supposed to hear court cases; these were still reserved for kiaps to handle, in the spirit of Native Affairs. Nevertheless, there was in practice enormous pressure on them to do so, especially since many of the just-elected councillors had earlier been *bosboi* or *luluai/tultuls*. The people expected councillors to handle 'big troubles' and their *komiti* to deal with smaller problems. If they failed to solve these, they could bring them to the councillor. In other words, an implicit hierarchy was erected, and it was assumed that this stretched in a linear fashion from the councillors to the government in general – a 'line of power', in fact (M. Strathern 1972; A. J. Strathern 1973). The kiaps, however, did not recognize this indigenous 'model'. For them, councillors were merely acting as informal mediators in civil cases, and their decisions could be overturned in court, while the people tended to view them as both big-men and government officials. Since the kiaps were quite likely to repudiate both images, this led to confusion and annoyance. If social control was effective, it was despite this hiatus of perception regarding the councillor's role. A feeling built up, therefore, during this period, that councillors were being denied the necessary powers to handle disputes. When kiaps were replaced by Local Court magistrates, the problems worsened rather than improved, because these magistrates did not go on patrol, and came to the Council Centre on one day of the week at the most. Litigants would therefore have to walk several miles often to get their case heard, and had no guarantee that it would be placed on the list. Further, magistrates were trained in introduced law rather than in custom, and this led to difficulties when they heard, for example, marriage cases.

There was, therefore, a strong felt need for the Village Courts when these were first introduced in 1976. The legislation behind them aimed at, first, allowing the people to choose their own magistrates and, second directing them to handle cases in accordance with customary principles. Professional lawyers were banned from taking part in Village Court proceedings, and the spirit of the legislation was to ensure that informal ways of dealing with disputes could flourish and also that the people would have regular access to justice. These aims were admirable, and have been realized in part. However, certain technical matters were overlooked or misjudged. No definite method of choosing magistrates was instituted, for example. Many were said to have been nominated by the local MP, working through the Council, without consulting the people in any formal manner. Court fines were supposed to be paid to the council clerks, but in practice magistrates tended to receive fines at the courthouses, and accusations arose that not all of the fine monies were passed on. Also, only one briefing session was held by a visiting lawyer, when the courts began, and it was impossible for new magistrates to absorb all that was said in the two-day session. Most significantly of all, few of the magistrates were literate, and tended to regard the handbook on types of cases and fines suggested for penalties as a formal instruction book on how to run the cases themselves. As a result, they were unduly dependent on the literate court clerks, who gained an inappropriately prominent place in the process of decision-making. At Tigi in Dei Council when the first courts were heard, for instance, magistrates turned to the clerk and asked what the fines were for insulting language or slander, and the clerks read out the maximum fine prescribed.[5] This was at once put into effect and charged, as though the magistrates had no flexibility at all. This was either a gross misunderstanding of the book or a deliberate drive to impose maximum fines so as to gain revenue, for it was early on understood that the magistrates' income depended on the collection of court fines. Where compensation was prescribed, the courts also added a fine component, so that some money always went into the 'government bank'.

While the aim of the legislation, then, was to 're-customize' the hearing of disputes, in effect this aim was illusory, since the previous 'customary' situation no longer existed. For the Village Courts to be effective, they had to be seen by Hageners as possessing the same kind of state-based legitimacy and power as the Local Courts and the police. Hence early on the Village Court Peace Officers demanded to have a uniform which would make them look much as possible like the national government's police force; they also wanted handcuffs to carry round. Court clerks also built dais-like desks at which they sat. Informal mediations were held outside rather than inside the courthouses, and once inside, people had to stand stiffly, much as they used to do in the 1960s when the kiap was around. Anyone talking loudly near the court-house was fined, and anyone trying to talk to those already 'gaoled', in the court ante-room, was charged with a criminal offence. Peace Officers threatened with sticks those who pressed their noses to window panes in order to look in at court proceedings, and constantly told plaintiffs and defendants alike to stand straight with their feet together. Despite all these attempts to make people respect the courts in bearing and behaviour, credit so gained was lost if a magistrate turned up drunk, gave blatantly biased decisions, heard cases involving his own relatives, or obviously absconded with court fine money. Dei Council has a chief Village Court magistrate, and he holds inspections and workshops for magistrates, so there are corrective devices built into the system. At Tigi, one magistrate was removed for drunkenness and replaced by another of the same clan, who soon showed himself as biased as his predecessor had been irresponsible, but who nevertheless remained in office. He presided over a case involving a lineage sister of his who wished to divorce her husband, and used his status to reduce the amount of bride-wealth returned to the husband. Actions such as this earned the Tigi court the sobriquet *kng-grit kot*, 'pig-grease court', and people said they would not use it. In the Kawelka clan area a move was made to have a separate court set up to service the Kawelka and some of the Minembi clans. It was rumoured that this move failed simply because an existing magistrate objected to it, but in fact the reason given by the Village Court Secretariat Office in Mt Hagen was shortage of money. A courthouse had in fact already been built at Golke School playground, and it stood forlorn and empty for the next two years, 1980–82, for no-one advised the people that they would have to renew their application regularly in order to secure a new court area from 1983–84 onwards. Discontent with the decisions of Tigi court led litigants to travel several miles to the administrative headquarters for

Hagen North District, "to which Dei as a whole belongs. Here, at Muglamp, the chief Village Court magistrate participates in sittings, and an Assistant District Commissioner also has his office nearby.

I have presented the Village Courts as suffering from problems of misunderstanding, affecting their legitimacy. It is also possible to argue, as Peter Fitzpatrick has done (1980), that they are in fact agencies of the emerging capitalist society, since they are generally staffed by men who are better off than the mass, who advocate strong penalties with heavy monetary fines for offenders. They become, that is, 'law and order' men, as opposed to 'rascals'. Indeed, during the 1970s the 'rascal' phenomenon began to invade even the Hagen countryside. Youths formed themselves into gangs, moving around at night, breaking into stores and seizing girls: an aspect of the urbaniz-ation of the countryside in which vehicles, store goods, beer, and social-night string bands all played their part.[6] It is hard to tell from this example whether Village Court magistrates acted primarily as con-cerned people, as conservatives, as capitalists, all three, or situationally as one or the other. Structurally, however, it is certainly significant that high fines were charged, and there is no doubt that the courts were seen by magistrates as revenue-raising agencies. In this sense, at least, they are unequivocally a part of the introduced legal-economic complex.

A point which must be stressed here, as earlier, is that *all* activities in the Highlands nowadays are of a 'mixed' character. When we say that Village Courts reflect the capitalist economic system, this does not exclude the fact that they are also influenced by customary ideas and that the actual decisions they make reflect cultural conceptions about the person, shame, responsibility, and so on. Emphatically, they do reflect these ideas, but it is still significant that these courts have ordered fines to be paid as well as, or instead of, compensation to injured or aggrieved parties, as already mentioned. This indicates that the magistrates quite self-consciously realize they are operating an introduced, state-based institution and not just deciding disputes by 'customary law'.

The same 'mixture' is to be seen in the activities of politicians. Since 1972 Dei Council has had the same MP, Mr Parua Kuri, a supporter of the United Party which has been a secondary partner in two successive government coalitions in the National Parliament. Parua has not held any ministerial positions, and while he began his career as a dynamic young leader able to hold his own with plantation owners and kiaps, he has since become a strong 'establishment' figure, in line with the general image of the United Party itself. Parua is a master of combining the rhetoric of development with full involvement in traditional-style politics. He is helped by being the son of a very famous big-man, whose own reputation, like that of Ongka-Kaepa in the allied Kawelka group, to Parua's Tipuka, was enhanced by the advent of Europeans and their shell wealth. Parua was also Vice-President and subsequently President of Dei Local Government Council prior to his election in 1972 and he has always retained his councillorship, thus preventing any rival from emerging within his own clan by this route. He has three wives and several grown-up children, most of them well-educated, and by 1982 there was talk that he would retire and allow his eldest son to stand for election in his place. He decided against this, however, and during his campaign hinted that if his traditional allies in Kawelka failed to vote for him he might hold up or renege on his returns for the huge *moka* gift which they had made to him in 1974 (see A. J. Strathern 1979b; the film *Ongka's Big Moka*). In addition, he was himself obliged to invest money in his campaign for the usual buying of beer and using his new vehicle to carry supporters; he said bluntly that in 1982 he was simply having to 'buy' votes. This gives us a parallel to the case of the Village Courts. When magistrates say that people must 'buy' large fines for their actions, whose interests are they defending? Similarly, when politicians say they must 'buy' votes, does this indicate that the whole operation has become undisguisedly commercial?

This is not quite the case, since it is evident that in fact votes cannot simply be bought in this way, otherwise it would always be the richest man who won. There is a tendency in this direction, but it is both masked and modified by the continuing pattern of segmentary allegiances between groups. These are subject to historical shifts, marked and in part generated by ceremonial transactions. In so far as these transactions nowadays involve the expenditure of money, it is evident that the whole political system is tied in with the new economic structures. Nevertheless, the segmentary allegiances are not just ideology, and no individual leader can 'buy' his way through them. Instead, what all politicians attempt to do is manipulate them, and Parua, for example, has had twenty years of experience in doing so.

It is also interesting to note that while Parua spoke privately of buying votes, in public he took his stand for renewed election on the grounds that while he was MP Dei Council had no 'trouble', that is no large-scale tribal fighting such as other parts of the Hagen area have chronically experienced. This was a powerful 'law and order' claim, again similar to those made for their functions by Village Court magistrates, and it is striking that what he did *not* claim was that as MP he had brought many development projects to his electorate, for indeed he had not. The rhetoric has changed markedly, then, since the 1960s, when the entire conception of the MP's role was that he should act as a super councillor, obtaining roads, schools, hospitals, aid posts, and other projects from the 'big government' in Port Moresby. It is the same with the Local Government Council, where unless one is on the finance committee such benefits cannot be steered in the direction of one's own group. At national level, this can be done only by or through ministers, and such moves can also often bring their own nemesis. In 1981–82 it became apparent that the Ministers for Commerce and Primary Industry, both United Party members, had used their positions in this way, and as a result both were removed from office. Through the Leadership Code, the Ombudsman Commission has the power to check on the business dealings of all politicians, and eventually corruption tends to be discovered.

In 1982 Parua experienced for the first time a challenge from a younger educated man in his own tribe, Mr Matrus Mel. Matrus determined that he would investigate Parua's use of some K30,000 of government money which he had received for handing out in his electorate to approved sectoral programmes in agriculture or transport. He belongs to a clan which had fought Parua's clan in the past, and Parua was alleged to have attempted to stop a scheme whereby this clan was to develop part of its land for cash-cropping, not far from where Parua himself has a long-standing development scheme. Veiled threats of sorcery accompanied these manoeuvres, and less veiled near-misses in vehicles driven by the two along narrow roads. Matrus attempted to use the party structure to gain financial backing. He had been an Economics student at the University of Papua New Guinea, but had no developed business base of his own. He also befriended Andrew Kei, a prominent businessman standing in the wider Western Highlands regional electorate; he visited the office of the People's Progress Party in Port Moresby; he was introduced both to the National and the Pangu Party élite in Hagen, and at one stage was endorsed by Pangu. However, eventually he was forced to stand as an Independent, without any real party support. For the Pangu Party in Mt Hagen was content to wait for the outcome and proposed persuading Parua to join them if he were the survivor, and if Raphael Ndoa of the United Party did not secure re-election at regional level. Parua hardly campaigned at all, in the sense of publicly defending his record or making new promises. His claim that thanks to him Dei was free of trouble was somewhat tarnished, however, when just before voting began in June, a serious conflict emerged between the Kombukjla and Roklaka groups (see Chapter 1).

In Pangia, the 'law and order' issue does not exist at the broad inter-group level, as I have noted at the beginning of this chapter. Moreover, the area is still short of actual development projects. However, a young graduate here also challenged the sitting United Party member, Mr Pundia-Kange. Correspondingly the sectoral programme funds issue was handled as a very serious matter, and Pundia's challenger tried to show he had attempted to benefit the area more than Pundia himself. The challenger, Mr Robert Paia, had the advantage of being approved by the Provincial Government in Mendi, for which he had worked as Cultural Officer, and in addition held a degree in social work and community development and had attempted for five years to improve access to cattle and poultry schemes in his own part of Pangia. He had also interested potential investors in plantation schemes throughout the rest of the area. Development was therefore the key issue preached in his campaign, and at one stage, when the Prime Minister visited Pangia, it was said that Pundia had told him that when Mr Somare, the previous PM, had visited, he brought K30,000 with him for the area's development. What, it was rhetorically asked, was Sir Julius Chan bringing now? The Prime Minister, for whose party Robert Paia was standing, replied, 'I will tell you that when you tell me what you did with the K40,000 we gave you earlier to bring here.' This interchange may have a folkloric appearance, but it is likely that it did in fact take place. Later, the national radio reported that Mr Paia had been attacked while attending a party hosted by Mr Kange: Robert Paia's car was stoned and he himself threatened. As in the case of Parua versus Matrus in Dei, intimations of violence were never far from the surface during this campaign, and Robert's supporters consistently claimed that Pundia's men had sworn to attack and kill him should he dare actually to stand for election. The Prime Minister next went on record deploring such threats, and promising they would be investigated and punished. In separate statements, he also urged that voters should not be bribed nor newly elected independent members be hustled into party affili-ations by those hungry for the Prime Ministership after the results were known.[8]

All these examples indicate the growing importance of politics in the Highlands, and reflect the fact that important material benefits flow from success in obtaining political office. It is necessary, therefore, to look at economic changes in order to understand how they have interacted with political ones.

The basic point is in line with Marxist theory on the penetration of capitalism into pre-capitalist structures. Politics has become 'commoditized'. In the 1960s candidates asked for votes on the grounds that they were 'good men' and 'strong men', well known for their ability to act as negotiators and thus to obtain general benefits for their electorate. During the 1970s there was growing emphasis on material wealth, on the prominent membership of development corporations, and the swinging of block votes behind these. In the 1982 elections a fully commoditized model emerged: candidates would buy votes and sitting MPs would use their sectoral programme funds covertly, in order to do this. This commoditization, then, reflects the growing importance of money as such in the economy of Highlands societies, money which is gained largely from growing coffee, and thus from changes in the system of basic production. This is the topic of the next chapter.

Notes

1 In 1982 University students and graduates standing in both Pangia and Dei Council fell far short of unseating the sitting United Party Members, Pundia-Kange and Parua-Kuri.
2 What was startling in the aftermath of the 1982 elections was the violence shown by supporters of defeated candidates, especially since these had been sitting members until their defeat. Hagen township was declared an emergency zone by police at the end of June after a government office was burnt down and several houses were broken into. Sadly, the house was the old District Office, which earlier had also been the residence of the first District Commissioner, and had been designated to become a new Cultural Centre by the Provincial Government. Pro-United, anti-Pangu Party people were supposed to have burnt it.
3 The kiap best remembered in this role for his energy and wise sayings was Roger Gleeson. Big-men still refer to their tussles with him and to some of his aphorisms; he has, in fact, achieved the honorary status of a big man whose advice and quips are quoted by others.
4 Yap also had the blessing of Ongka, the influential older leader. Ongka supplied a catch-phrase for him: 'Our people only go past the *kang röprö*, they do not see the *porembil.*' The reference is to the Female Spirit cult, in which non-participants only go through the first fence called 'the boys' fence', whereas the men who are cult celebrants proper go further and see the

upright stake that marks the Spirit. Here the 'boys' fence' is the open Council meetings, while the *porembil* is the finance committee.

5 See Appendix 1. This was an initial field report prepared in late 1977 soon after the courts were instituted in Dei, and as such requires some updating. Basically, the new court system has fully established itself as the prime means whereby disputes are to be settled, but it still suffers from many of the problems which became evident at its inception. The trend of its development in Dei has been towards greater formalization. Peace Officers have uniforms and handcuffs, and the courts have their own vehicle with a lock-up area at the back in which convicted persons who are to go to jail are transported. While a lone remaining kiap in 1979 was suggesting that perhaps magistrates should be hearing cases under trees in settlements and working on foot ('appropriate legal technology'), the MP and magistrates themselves were urging that courts only be heard inside closed permanent-materials buildings, to which the public had no direct access. For a general discussion relevant to this type of process, see Fitzpatrick 1980.

6 At the time of the 1982 elections, the actions of such 'rascals' increased sharply throughout the Western Highlands Province. Earlier in the year two research workers had found they were surrounded by a crowd of threatening young men in the Wurup area, and as a result had to abandon their project. A Yamka family from Keluwa near Mt Hagen was notorious in this regard, and their gang leader, John Peng, was credited with access to unusually powerful guns and a super-charged sports car which could outrun any police vehicle. Mr Peng was caught and convicted on a murder charge, against which he appealed in mid-1982. He later 'repented' and became a 'born-again' Christian of the Pentecostal church.

7 *Ongka's Big Moka* was produced by Charlie Nairn for the Granada Television series 'Disappearing World' and was first shown in 1974.

8 Mr Ndoa had earlier advised me that Mr Kange would win, and he in fact did so by a large margin.

5 Production

In the preceding chapters I have argued that pacification, missioniz-ation, and the introduction of new political roles have all had their effects in Hagen and Pangia, leading to rather different outcomes in the two areas. The question now arises as to how such changes are linked with any alterations in productive activities. This is obviously crucial to the discussion broached in Chapter 1, in which I voiced scepticism concerning the orthodox Marxist view of the relationship between base and superstructure. In an effort to bypass the compelling metaphorical bias of the terms 'base' and 'superstructure' themselves, I have adopted instead a constrast between 'cultural' and 'sociological' factors, leaving open the matter of how these are to be related in analysis.

Discussions of production are usually conducted in an etic, sociologi-cal vein. No matter how much the 'indigenous model' may be respected if one is dealing with religion, say, or kinship, when it comes to pro-duction such actor-based perspectives are pushed aside in favour of a strictly quantitative approach based on energy flows, labour time, or whatever factor is uppermost in the analytical scheme of the author.

This is an error, because it perpetuates the metaphor of base and super-structure and somehow privileges the realm of production as a special case outside 'culture'.

This is not to suggest that observer-created analytical schemes are invariably wrong; it is simply to sound a warning that counting things does not in itself automatically produce an objective social science. The theoretical framework has always to be constructed in association with such quantitative exercises, and the relationship between framework and data is complicated. This is so for the question of 'relations of pro-duction' which many writers interested in a neo-Marxist anthropology have taken as their central interest. The concept bridges superstructure and base since it deals with production, but also refers to the social forms by which production takes place. Further, extra-cultural factors called 'forces of production' preserve the purity of the base from inter-ference by the cultural level, such that crucial change in the mode of production is said to occur only when the forces of production have reached a certain level – despite the fact that in the Soviet Union itself the actual historical events reversed this priority: political revolution took place first, and the forces of production were altered later.

Nevertheless, this rather cumbersome distinction between forces and relations does have some merit, and can be used to elucidate certain aspects of change in Highlands societies. For example, there is little doubt that the introduction of the sweet potato into the Highlands some 300 or 400 years ago did significantly alter its societies. The alter-ation did not consistitute the type of 'revolution' which J. B. Watson originally proposed; but it did speed up processes such as the intensifi-cation of agriculture and population growth, setting the scene for an extreme contemporary contrast between central and fringe Highlands societies. As it happens, and for reasons which are not fortuitous, this contrast has been further strengthened by the processes of colonial change and economic development. The first explorers moved into places where there were large populations and where airstrips could be made in grasslands to take light planes. These same populations built the airstrips, and later, roads that opened up their societies to the out-side world. And it was these societies that developed a particularly strong interest in the types of shell valuables that the Europeans brought. Sweet potato was converted into pigs, and pigs into shells, which stood at the pinnacle of prestige-creation in Hagen, being especially associated with big men and their prominence in *moka*. The rate at which such conversions could proceed was stimulated originally by the arrival of sweet potato, since this enabled more pigs to be kept and gardens to be made at higher altitudes.

But as with all such arguments, it cannot be said that this particular crop in itself caused the Highlands social systems to develop in the way they did. Sweet potato was adopted into an existing agricultural system based on taro cultivation, and merely *allowed* a higher level of production if this was considered desirable. Such desirability in turn depends on specified political aims. It is possible, of course, to say that humans have a constant propensity to maximize their own reproduction (the basic hypothesis of socio-biology), and that this is the basic force which impels them to technical innovation under favourable circumstances. Hence if a new crop becomes available, the population will rise to make use of its new resource. This argument, however, is too simple. Even if such a propensity does exist (and it seems probable that in fact it does), this does not mean that it will always find equal expression in every culture, or that it may not be overridden by other considerations. Balancing mechanisms are clearly required, since an unchecked propensity of this kind would rapidly lead to any population outrunning its resources and thus facing starvation rather than maximum reproductive success. The basic defect of the socio-biological hypothesis used by itself alone is that it ignores the fact that human beings also seem to have a propensity to live in groups, which then oppose other similar groups around them, so that human history always has a political dimension derived from group living. Thus, in the Highlands, if sweet potato had an effect, this was mediated through and in turn influenced an existing set of political relations between groups. It is quite possible that some of the existing named, large segmentary groups came into being during the sweet potato era, but it is unlikely that the Highlands cultures as such are so recent in time depth, since their languages certainly show a period of some 10,000 years of divergence from possible prototype forms. Golson's archaeological work at Kuk in the Western Highlands (in territory traditionally owned by the Kawelka people) shows that there, in the swamp basin, agriculture goes back some 9,000 years, and it is reasonable to suppose that this period may coincide with the birth and development of major Highlands languages, with their associated cultures (Golson 1982). Kuk may from very early on, then, have been a centre of innovation, which drew in trade goods and tools from elsewhere, including pearl shells from the Southern Highlands, nassa shells from the Jimi Valley to the north, and axes from factories at Aviamp and Dom to the east.[1] It is also possible that prototypical forms of big-manship were elaborated during the long period of reliance on taro and bananas, and that these were *not* uniformly diffused in wider areas until the time of sweet potato. The very widespread story of the volcanic ash fall sometimes ends, as in an Enga version, by telling how after the fall a new 'race' of people appeared, and crops flourished unusually well so that the population expanded. Since the last ash fall in fact occurred some 300 years ago, according to the finds at Kuk, this view may be quite close to the historical truth, since it was about this time that sweet potato came (Blong 1982).

A question hardly broached in the literature is exactly *how* did the sweet potato 'come'? Birds sometimes carry seeds and drop them in faeces elsewhere; new varieties of sweet potato are in fact spread in this way, so the plant itself may have originally come in like manner (Bulmer 1966). But it is also possible that it was purposefully brought in by groups of people, and that these could have displaced or incorporated earlier groups. In this way a new 'race' of people might be faintly remembered in oral traditions.

It is also important to note here that the sweet potato did not turn the Highlands into a simple monocrop region. Sweet potato does predominate in most places, least in environments such as that of the Maring and Karam, north of the Jimi, and most in places such as Jobakogl in Upper Chimbu where little else can be grown apart from sugar-cane, but the older crops are always retained. This is neatly seen in the terms for garden in the Melpa language. They are *pana* and *okapana* (or *pona* in C. Melpa: I give N. Melpa forms). *Pana* is evidently the general term, yet it in practice refers to mixed vegetable gardens in which greens, bananas, sugar-cane, and taro are grown together; *oka pana* is the sweet potato garden. I suggest that *pana* is indeed the ancient term and that in pre-Ipomoean times *pana* gardens contained much the same plants as they do now. This was how 'gardens' in general were. Monocrop horticulture developed with the late arrival of sweet potato, at which time the term *oka-pana* would have been coined.[2] As Waddell has suggested, the extent to which there is a definite split between sweet potato gardens and others is an index of the degree to which there is an intensification of emphasis on rearing pigs for festivals. Among the Tsembaga, Waddell's proposition takes on a cyclical form: sweet potato gardens are expanded to feed the herd of pigs, and decline after the pig kill is over, allowing the taro-yam (*dangwan-duk*) gardens to again predominate (Waddell 1972; Rappaport 1968).

Another point which has been suggested as correlated with the relatively recent appearance of sweet potato is that magic to make it grow well is not very predominant. More ritual and magic always seem to attach to taro and yams. This is certainly true in Hagen. Sweet potato there is a means to an end, human and porcine subsistence, and ritual attaches to the pig itself rather than to the crop on which the pig lives. Thus there is magic for increasing the size of litters carried by sows, and for enlarging the areas of subcutaneous fat in pigs being raised for *moka*. There is magic to make taro grow, controlled mostly by women, since it is women who do the taro planting. Women also, of course, are in charge of planting the sweet potato vines, but it is worth noting that the process of planting and harvesting this crop is continuous, and a woman may simply push back a few vines into the ground after she has taken some tubers. Taro, by contrast, is a corm, and when harvested its top must be preserved for replanting. There is thus more of a sense of the death and rebirth of the plant itself, involved in the recycling of its shoots. It may be that for this reason taro has been seen as a suitable vehicle for symbolic values, for instance, as among the Orokaiva of Oro Province outside of the Highlands region, or in the Baktaman, Western Province, and the Telefomin area of West Sepik Province (Schwimmer 1973; Barth 1975). But another point arises when we look at the situation in Pangia, where there is in fact magic for the growth of all kinds of crops, including sweet potato itself. Taro is still a special rather than a subsistence crop here, and formerly it was grown with great care by men and used as a form of gift in exchanges. (Crops are not used in this way in Hagen, that is, are not presented raw as gifts, except at funerals, when sweet potato and sugar-cane are usually given by sympathetic kin to the principal mourners.) Sweet potato is the staple, as it is in Hagen, but there is magic both to make tubers grow well and to entice away those from another person's garden so that they enter one's own. The latter form is operated by jealous co-wives. As one woman put it:

'We have *man* (magic) for stealing the sweet potato from a co-wife's garden section. You plant one of your own vines in her area and you say a spell, and all the nodes on which tubers form come into your own section. The other woman's plot bears leaves but no tubers, and then she will fight you over this. She may counter by first making another spell to fix her plants in her own garden. But her rival may secretly pull up her vines and throw them into water, then replace them with ones of her own. Then, no tubers will form, and the two will fight.'   (Information from Wembi-Kumbea 1982)

This ethnographic contrast raises questions similar to those originally broached by Malinowski in his comparison between lagoon and open-sea fishing in the Trobriands. He argued that magic originates in anxiety and so if conditions are secure and the catch is assured, magic will not be employed (Malinowski 1948). Radcliffe-Brown, of course, turned Malinowski's argument upside down by arguing that magic and ritual may produce, rather than proceed from, anxiety (Radcliffe-Brown 1952). In both areas under consideration there is suspicion and competition between co-wives, and they suspect one another of making magic to secure the interest and affections of their shared husband while excluding the others. So, anxiety certainly exists and this correlates with the use of competitive magic. But in Hagen there is still no sweet potato magic. What factors, then, differentiate the two cases?

In both areas, men often prepare a single garden, which they divide between a number of women, typically co-wives. The divisions are marked by heaps of rubbish, trenches, lengths of timber, or red cordyline plants which remain after the garden is exhausted, and in theory determine how it will be used again next time. It is therefore quite feasible for women to intrude on each other's sections, if no-one is watching. In Hagen, women sometimes angrily accuse one another of digging up crops outside their own plots or of letting their pigs get in. Is it only fortuitous, then, that they do not also possess magic to steal one another's tubers? Perhaps, but as it happens there are indications that two further factors are also involved: one is that in Pangia women have stronger claims over their own products than in Hagen and are more prepared to assert such claims; the second is that the subsistence cropping in Pangia does not appear to be as secure as in Hagen. It is hard to tell whether this is a result of colonial influence, and certainly the situation was exacerbated in the 1960s by government practices, since numbers of young men were removed to work on plantations elsewhere and the people who remained were forced to contribute their unpaid labour to government and mission projects as well as maintaining their own gardens. Two severe periods of frost in 1972 and 1977 resulted in destruction of sweet potato gardens, but reports of food shortages were not confined to these dates. Rather, they occur regularly in patrol reports, from 1960 onwards. Further, such shortages are definitely remembered from pre-contact times, and the names of wild plants sought and consumed in these temporary famines are a part of folk knowledge to an extent unknown in Hagen. Sweet potato tubers in Tunda village in 1967 were definitely smaller and harvests poorer than among the Kawelka in Dei Council, and Pangia people who visited Hagen made the same observation. Rainfall in Pangia is on average twice as heavy as in Hagen, although altitude is consistently lower (between 3,000 ft and 5,500 ft above sea level as compared with 5,500 ft and 7,000 ft). Tubers rot in the fields, and are attacked by rats, which also infest the piles of rubbish used as internal section-markers. The grid-iron pattern of trenching practised in Hagen, which is designed to allow quick drainage, is not used in Pangia. Instead, a form of mounding has been adopted, which clearly owes its origins to the much higher-altitude areas to the north, Ialibu and Tambul, and is primarily designed to enhance fertility and protect tubers against the cold rather than to maximize water run-off. Mounding is done at Tunda in well-established sweet potato gardens after a first full planting and harvesting has been completed and the ground is considered soft enough to work in this way. Men make mounds with steel spades, women with digging sticks and their hands. South of Tunda mounding is not carried out at all, and sweet potato is simply planted in large untrenched garden plots along with corn and patches of taro.

In short, techniques for maximizing sweet potato yields are not highly-developed in Pangia. Fencing also tends to be less stout and it therefore rots with heavy rain, allowing pigs to enter and disturb tuber growth. This in turn leads to a persistent pattern of litigation over crop damage caused by pigs, marked by demands that the guilty pigs be shot. Kiaps in the 1960s discouraged people from keeping pigs in their own houses, as they had done in the past. Instead, they were to be kept at night in stalls constructed outside the village, or they simply slept in the bush. As a result, the pigs became less domesticated. They were not cross-bred with introduced European strains as they were in Hagen. Since people, both men and women, had to spend time on government work, they had less time to make adequate gardens for themselves and their pigs. Also, in Pangia male pigs are not systematically castrated as they are in Hagen. They are allowed to grow up and mate once or twice with the pigs around them, including, informants add, their mothers and sisters, before their testicles are removed. There are therefore large numbers of aggressive young male pigs about. In Hagen more pigs are castrated early on, and special boars are kept which serve the sows of the clan, their owners receiving a fee for this expenditure of semen. The owner keeps his boar penned in, and after a few years raises another boar and castrates the old one, allowing it to grow fat. All these factors combine to produce greater losses of garden crops in Pangia. Finally, new varieties of sweet potato seem to have found their way into Hagen more often, and these usually offer advantages in terms of yields, tuber size, or even nutritional content. It is reasonable to suppose that crops travelled along the same routes as objects used in trade. Hagen and Wahgi commanded access to stone axe factories, whereas the Pangia area did not. It is therefore also likely that there were more stone axes available per worker in Hagen and this would also enable production to be boosted there, although this factor of difference would tend to disappear when steel axes became widely available. The supply of stone work axes is certainly a factor of production belonging to the realm of 'forces' rather than 'relations', although it is also to be noted that such axes were in the past distributed from the factories through affinal links and thus their entry into productive activities was governed by the same structures of kinship and exchange which feature as relations of production in general.

The gist of my argument so far is simple. For definite material reasons, Hagen had an advantage in productive terms over Pangia, and this is reflected even nowadays when steel tools are used in both places. It is also reflected, I have speculatively suggested, in the use of competitive magic by rival co-wives in Pangia to appropriate sweet potato tubers.

I have also noted that in Pangia women have perhaps a stronger conceptual control over their own products, whether these be crops, artefacts, pigs, or children. This is a consistent cultural trait, and is certainly not an immediate precipitate of material factors. It has a logical fit with the pattern of attempting to extend such control magically to the products of a rival who in a sense is symbolically conflated with oneself. But it is also possible that there is a more general matter at issue here. In Hagen, the development of the *moka* system has led to a progressive distinction between production and transaction and has given, as Marilyn Strathern (1978) has shown, a twist to gender relations such that female : male : : production : transaction. As a necessary concomitant of this process, when products of labour are defined as entering transactions, they are labelled as under the control of men and therefore removed from women. This structural separation has not occurred, or not to the same degree, in all Highlands systems, and it marks a sharp difference between Pangia and Hagen. In Pangia not only is the major nexus of gift-giving the matrilateral complex of kin ties, but male actors are pulled into this in such a way as to conflate them with females, and vice versa. The sexes are thus seen as more mutually substitutable than in Hagen, and by the same token they are conceptually more equal. It therefore follows that women have a strong claim over what they produce, just as men do. For example, they give *langi* gifts of food to kin, which are reciprocated with shells, and these they give to their husbands to use in payments for their jointly created children or for themselves. A claim over products does not mean that a woman is unconstrained; as an actor in exchanges she incurs an obligation to give and receive as men do. I do not think, either, that this situation of Wiru women is necessarily a result of the particular levels of production reached in Pangia by comparison with Hagen. No doubt, there are areas of medium-intensity production (perhaps the Daribi) where women's roles in exchange differ again from those of Wiru women (Wagner 1967). The symbolic construction of persons as social actors is thus not simply a precipitate of factors of technology and production; the point is that one always finds several factors bound together. As it happens, in Hagen production is more intensive than it is in Pangia, but there are also social structural differences between the two, and it is doubtful if these are all historically the result of different intensity of land use.

Another question now arises. Elsewhere in the Highlands government and mission officials have had a considerable impact on gender relations, not always in consistent directions. Thus missions disapprove of promiscuity and usually also of pagan courting practices such as the Melpa 'head turning' ceremony, or traditional forms of self-decoration in which the person's body is revealed and enhanced. This policy tends, therefore, to be repressive towards both sexes. Government officers, however, have tended to support the rights of women, at least in so far as divorce and the custody of children is concerned. Marie Reay reports that in Minj at one stage the rule *laik bilong meri* ('a woman's wish') began to predominate in court cases over marriage, largely because the kiaps instigated and encouraged it. Since kiaps were very dominant in Pangia in the 1960s it is possible that they instituted a similar historical phase there, and that the difference between Hagen and Pangia women's 'status' (using the term simply as a shorthand form here) is merely a result of recent history. However, I do not think so. Kiaps are no longer dominant, and though their mantle and some of their power have devolved on to Village Court magistrates there is little evidence of the *laik bilong meri* syndrome as such in the handling of court cases.

But a Wiru woman's claims to her gardens crops, pigs, and children are very firm and are also respected in court. This strongly corroborates the view that such claims are structurally based and are not recent innovations. Wiru women also use the introduced steel tools, axes, bush knives, and spades, more readily than do Hagen women, a point which also suggests a less extreme gender differentiation.

The basic sexual division of labour is nevertheless similar and is linked to ideas about land-holding. In both areas land-holders are usually thought of as men. In 1967 I enquired as to the owners of gardens in all the sites around Tunda village, and invariably the (admittedly male) informants gave the names of men. Men mark their ownership by deciding when to open a garden for use or re-use; by fencing and perhaps ditching its perimeter; by clearing it of grass, rushes, and timber; and finally apportioning it to females for actual planting. They also generally plant sugar-cane and bananas, and they specialize or specialized in growing fine types of taro and fruit pandanus. Women grow all manner of greens, beans, and sweet potatoes. Corn is planted by both sexes (note that it is an early colonial import into the Highlands). A basic rule which also holds for both areas is that the planter has the prime claim over what is planted. Hence women gain control over vegetable crops for which they are responsible. This rule has carried over into the era of cash, so that women see it as their right to harvest and market their crops and to keep the money if they have planted what they sell. Both men and women take crops to market, but women predominate, and when men are the sellers their wares are normally the bananas, sugar-cane, and introduced crops such as peanuts and cabbages which they have planted. Here is a case, then, where a certain kind of labour input (planting) brings with it the right to control disposal of the product. Conversely, if one disposes of something which one has not planted, the cash belongs to the planter rather than to oneself. The situation arises most often when men tell their wives in Hagen to market sugar-cane for them, expecting to receive the proceeds. Sugar-cane is heavy to carry and the wife in turn expects to be given a share of the money. If she is not, this creates bad feeling between those concerned, or reflects its prior existence (A. J. Srathern 1982a).

The same rules apply to the major cash crop, coffee. It, however, is an important resource, and men are most insistent that the coffee trees are theirs. They use the argument that the ground in which the trees are planted is theirs, because wives come to live with them on their clan land. In addition, men usually plant the actual trees themselves. Most of the planting was carried out in the 1960s and early 1970s, so that families have established plots which have been yielding for several years. In the 1960s also, agricultural officers quite often visited small-holders and advised on spacing, soil types, pruning, leaf diseases, shade trees, and the like. In Pangia they established nurseries for coffee seedlings and distributed these on request. Coffee planting and marketing is much more established in Hagen than in Pangia, how-ever, because heavy rainfall, poor site choices, and the poor condition of the Wiru road all conspire either to depress production or to discourage buyers from visiting the latter area. Department of Primary Industry officers themselves did buying rounds in the 1970s, but the Pangia people felt that the prices they offered were inferior. This was probably true in the sense that the prices were below what was paid for first class dry coffee beans at the coffee factory in Hagen town, because in Pangia coffee is difficult to dry and the cost of collecting it is high. Coffee prices also fluctuate from season to season, as vegetable crop prices do not, at least in the markets, and although people are well aware of this and of its supposed cause (the world market) they also suspect the buyers of tricking them by paying less than their company has set as the proper price, and pocketing the difference.[3]

Another matter of importance is the way in which coffee has been fitted into existing garden arrangements. In Hagen coffee was planted in *pana* garden sites, that is in the mixed vegetable areas where 'female' and 'male' crops were interspersed, the 'female' crops being harvested first, the 'male' crop later. Coffee seedlings were protected from the hot sun by small 'hats' of grass supported by a tripod of sticks, and as the crops grew and matured the garden would be gradually cleared, until after two years only the coffee plants remained; another two years and they bore fruit. Both sexes have given up valuable garden space in order to allow for coffee; but it is the men who make the strongest claim to the coffee beans themselves. Further, women have lost some of the land in which they grew nutritious greens, valuable for young children, and from which a surplus could also be sold in the market. Women depend on men, according to the conventional division of labour, to clear the ground for *pana* gardens. They cannot take axe and spade and cut a bush area themselves, because they do not hold the requisite land claims to do so. Men are also the ones who plant the casuarina trees which help to improve soil fertility, and assist in fixing their claims to the garden itself. They plant cordyline boundary markers. Their jural entitlements are clearly stressed against those of women.

In Pangia the situation is not quite the same. Sweet potato gardens often contain clumps of *Rungia klosii*, a favourite green which gives its name to green vegetables in general (*pingi*); corn is also planted. The special gardens for greens and sugar-cane tend to be made rather far from the settlements and are cut from forest or made from very old fallow ground; they are called *lama ipe*, 'forest gardens'. Coffee has not been planted in these because it would be inconvenient to care for it and protect the beans from theft at a distance from home. Instead, it has mostly been situated close to the houses themselves, and both sexes work at its harvesting and drying, old people being deputed to watch over it as it lies in the sun. It has not displaced any particular kind of garden, nor has it deprived women of an independent source of income. In any case, markets are not so well developed in Pangia, and women do not therefore earn as much from vegetables sales as they do in Hagen. It is not surprising, then, that conflict over the use of money has not developed so clearly there. Men also have less access to beer in Pangia, and until very recently did not travel regularly to Hagen. Since 1980, however, several men have bought twelve-seater buses which operate a service on the 112-kilometre route between Pangia Station and Hagen town. For the villages close to the Station itself, life is taking on more of the urban-influenced traits which are common throughout the Hagen area. Women from these villages have also married out to distant parts of the Western Highlands and beyond, and when pig kills are held cars visit from all over the Highlands. The station itself has a drinking club owned by a man from Kauwo, probably the most accul- turated village (in this sense) in Pangia. It was from Kauwo that the land for Pangia Station was purchased; the Lutheran mission at Tiripini and the new Pentecostal church are on its territory; it has a high pro- portion of trade stores, educated men, and vehicle owners; and a selection of its women have since 1960 made a living from sexual services performed for Station residents, an innovation strictly banned in those villages which are under the sway of the Evangelical Bible Mission or the Wesleyans.

There is one respect, however, in which the Pangia agricultural system was upset by colonial influence, and this did affect women. This was the removal of young men, both single and married, to work on the coast as labourers under the Highlands Labour Scheme. The scheme had also, of course, taken Hageners earlier, mostly in the 1950s, before much small-holder coffee growing had developed. Hagen labourers also helped to develop Goroka at this time, and were paid in pearl shells rather than cash. By the 1960s they were refusing to travel as contract labourers, however, both because their own coffee seedlings were growing and because they could earn extra cash by casual picking work on the coffee plantations established by expatriates throughout the Western Highlands. The search for labourers extended strongly to the newly-opened parts of the Southern Highlands, including Pangia. Men were airlifted out to Mendi or Hagen and allocated a plantation either on the northern coast (e.g., New Britain) or the southern (the hinterlands of Port Moresby). Roads were not necessary for the scheme to work; indeed it worked better without them, since when they were built young men tended to migrate independently along them to destinations of their own choice within the Highlands, rather than directly to Rabaul or Port Moresby. Having earned money in casual work, they then either bought tickets to fly to a major town or returned home by vehicle or on foot.

With regard to the impact of migration on gardening and pig rearing at home, in Pangia the removal of young men in this way *coincided in time* with strong government pressure on the people to do community work, run Council projects, build and support schools, attend baptismal classes, join women's clubs, construct government out-stations, and clear land for cattle projects. Even if the labour power of young men was surplus to the subsistence requirements in the past, it was precisely their presence that would have eased the burden on others faced with the variety of tasks demanded by the government officers in a village. It is true that one could argue that a certain amount of extra male labour power was released with the ending of warfare and the introduction of steel tools, and that this should be balanced against the demands of government work. Such an argument is, however, difficult to pursue, because the factors involved cannot very accurately be quantified. Further, even if they could, this would not settle the issue, because the division of labour is such that female and male labour has to be mixed in the work of production, just as in that of reproduction, and the expectation is that tasks are carried out jointly by wife and husband. If the husband is absent, a wife must depend on her in-laws for assistance or else she has to return to her own parents' place. In either case it is to the senior generation that she must ordinarily look for practical help, and if they are sick or too old they cannot fill the gap left by the husband. The amount of money which contract labourers brought back with them was never enough for a wife and family to live on when the man returned for a second period of work, as often happened. In one semi-mythical case, a wife is said to have complained to the resident kiap that her husband came home between contracts and stayed only long enough to make her pregnant again. The contracts tended to last for two years, so she was left always with a young baby to care for and no husband to assist her. She is said to have asked the kiap if he could make an order for her husband's testicles to be removed. He was unable to effect this, but is said to have put the husband in gaol for two months instead, an action which would have helped swell the Station labour force but would not have solved the wife's immediate problems. It was during this period that the pattern of pigs breaking into gardens became most severe. All women raise them, being very strongly motivated to do so because pork circulates largely in gifts to maternal kin. A woman can cope with up to ten pigs of varying sizes, but only if she is supported by her husband, for he has to supply pig ropes, stalls, and tethering posts, and to assist in carrying the tubers which the wife has dug up during the day in her garden for the animals to eat in the evenings. Without regular male help, a woman could not feed as many pigs, yet she would also not wish to kill those entrusted to her since they would be required for the next pig kill, and she would therefore be caught in a 'pig trap'. The pigs, for their part, would become hungry and break into gardens, further damaging the gardens' productive capacity. A downward cycle of production could thus be expected, and relief would not come until the husband returned and the pig population was reduced. One occasion when it is justified to kill a pig is when a sacrifice is needed as a part of the treatment for sickness. The strain on women and children may have produced the sicknesses and thus contained the demands of the pigs, but this is mere speculation. There is some evidence that in Pangia pigs are in any case let into gardens to root at an earlier stage than in Hagen, thus gaining a taste for digging up tubers for themselves. If this is true, it may be related to the lesser availability of rich fallow where pigs can forage for worms, frogs, and other small creatures. Or perhaps the practice is only recent and results from the crisis in the management of garden production which was precipitated by colonial policy in the 1960s, one which resulted in a paradoxical attempt by kiaps to remedy the situation by ordering the people to do garden work on Thursdays and Fridays and even sending uniformed policemen to check on this. Pangia in the late 1960s was certainly a police-dominated area, and people went in fear of police inspections and also attempted to manipulate friendly connections with them in order to have their rivals and enemies put in gaol. Occasionally there was a reaction. On one occasion in Tunda the police checked all the outside latrines, declared many unfit for use and hauled their owners off to court. Some of the younger men declared that the police had pushed roughly at the houses and had also cut vine supports. They raced to the Station with a twist of vines for evidence, hoping that the kiap might discipline his own officers. The investigation was inconclusive, and the policeman, from Gulf District, remained in his position.

The real problem of cash cropping in Pangia so far has been how to make it profitable. This is as true of the elaborate cattle schemes begun in 1967 with Development Bank backing as for small-holder coffee growing. These schemes were designed on a community basis, and were introduced by kiaps on patrol to every village. Both sexes performed the labour required to clear and fence large tracts of fallow land. A kind of division of labour was maintained since men did the fencing, with barbed wire and sawn posts, while women cut the undergrowth with bush knives in hope of a better pasture developing. A *bosboi* appointed by the kiap was made overseer of each project, receiving training also as 'cowboys' at the Baiyer River government stock farm in the Western Highlands. The idea was that each village would have its cows, and any meat sales would go first to repay the bank loan, and then to meet the costs of fencing materials, with any profit being recorded in a savings account book kept by the Local Government councillor for the group. Cattle were to be slaughtered only at Pangia Station and by Department of Agriculture personnel, for reasons of hygiene, so most of the meat would be sold to Station workers. Purchase of pieces for re-sale by project participants themselves was actually discouraged in what seems a peculiarly irrational piece of government policy. But these rules could have been tolerated if the projects brought in money. As it was, the Tunda scheme suffered problems. Pasture was poor and infested with a poisonous plant known as *wiringou*. People grew very tired of the work. Cattle became sick and died, and as each village owned only a few, each animal represented a large portion of its investment. Nor did the stock replenish itself by breeding, as pigs did, since bulls were not at first brought in. The poor pasture was further damaged by cattle hooves, and the high rainfall turned it into muddy pools separated by areas of brake. Pigs gradually made their way back into the project areas and churned them up further.

The next idea was to convert the large community projects into smaller, individually-owned ones, by placing new fences across the old pastures and by encouraging the clearing of new land by enterprising individuals. The problem was that the sheer amount of labour required to make new ranches was a severe discouragement to individuals. Those who could mobilize the necessary labour were later faced with the question of remuneration. So cattle schemes combined contradictory requirements: communal labour, followed by individual management and profit-making. Where ownership remained communal, profits were not made, nor indeed; if they had been, was there any definite idea of how to share them other than by re-investing in stock. Where individual ownership was adopted, labour to maintain the project was in short supply, or else had to be paid for by giving workers a share in the cattle, thus turning the project back into a communal one.

The Hagen experience with cattle schemes was not so traumatic, for two reasons. First, big, communal projects were not launched, and where smaller projects were started, they tended to be run by men who already had other income, as businessmen, politicians, or both. Second, the owners established a practice of selling live cows for use in *moka* exchanges, enabling the meat to be redistributed widely at the rural level and the owners to obtain immediate cash returns without paying for transport and slaughtering costs. Slaughtering was done at the Korn Farm station of the Department of Agriculture and the meat sold from there to town shops, but less money was generated from each cow by this method. It is the same with pigs: a live pig fetches more than the same one cooked and cut into pieces for the market. Economies of scale are needed before bulk production of meat for market can be profitable, a point which was realized by an expatriate entrepreneur who set up a huge ranch at Ruti in the Jimi Valley just before Independence. This has an outlet, its own butcher shop in Hagen town, and is very successful. The individual cattle schemes have now ceased to attract the attention of the more enterprising men, who instead are making riches for themselves in the takeover of coffee and tea plantations and real estate in and near the town.

A minor version of this process is taking place at Pangia, where leases over government land in the station area itself are eagerly contested, and prices for improved and unimproved areas of customary land nearby have rocketed to more than K1,000 per acre, where buyers can be found. Land owners claim that buyers will eventually do business and make huge profits, so they want their own compensation to be generous. They do not concede that business is uncertain and requires heavy borrowing in its initial stages. It seems likely that this attitude will either inhibit sales of customary land, or, alternatively lead to endless subsequent arguments about titles to land for development. At least one such dispute already exists, predictably involving a store built by a man from Maiya village on land owned by a Kauwo man, these two villages being traditional enemies.[4] The Kauwo man claims that the Maiya one made no initial payment for the use of the land and that he has obtained adequate profits, so has no more claims on improvements made. Allegedly K7,000 was promised as a payment after five years, but he gave up and took away his stock well before this. However, now that the land owner is trying to sell the assets plus ground for some K7,000, the Maiya man is filing a counter-suit, with the support from the sitting MP, Mr Pundia-Kange. Nearby, the Pondi village people have also made claims against Kauwo men to land beside a new high school built with funds from a World Bank grant, and won their case. One may expect that such disputes will escalate. Indeed, Pangia people are litigious over land just as they are over pigs, sexual behaviour, fruit pandanus trees, house sites, personal insults, and community work. The land disputes of the past also mostly reflected political alignments in warfare. Thus Tunda had boundary disputes with Marapini and Mamuane villages, and Kerepali, a village within the Tunda complex, had one with the Tawindi people of Kalue village. This flares up regularly, and relates to an area of potentially fertile forest land on a crest between the two villages. In the late 1970s it led to actual skirmishing, with subsequent arrests by police. There is little doubt that the heat generated in this matter resulted both from the opposition of enemy groups and from the perceived value of good forest land as a source of timber and new vegetable crops: the usual combination of old and new reasons, with a strong undercurrent of both ideological and material factors.

A similar sharpening of old disputes in a new context lies behind the much wider-scale tribal fighting of the Western Highlands. In each recorded case there has been a previous basis for enmity, as between the Ndika and Yamka near Hagen town, renewed by either a land dispute, a car accident, or a sorcery charge. One cannot say in a simple manner that 'land shortage' is the single cause of these troubles; but the revaluation of land as a source of revenue plus the selective acquisition of land by new business groups both greatly increase the tensions between rival groups. When in 1968 Mr Iambakey Okuk first came to Dei Council to campaign for the regional seat for the Western Highlands, he told his astonished audience through his loud-hailer that the white plantation 'masters and missuses' were all lying to them by claiming that Papua New Guineans could not take over these assets because they lacked the knowledge to run them. Old men muttered and said 'Can we believe this youth?' However, over the next few years the plantation acquisition scheme began and by 1981 not a single one in the Hagen area of the Western Highlands remained under expatriate ownership. All were taken over by business groups whose membership was founded on neo-traditional coalition-style ties between existing large groups. The three chief ones are the Pipilka Development Corporation, the Welyi-Kuta business group, and the Raembka, an alliance of Tipuka, Kawelka, and Nelka interests. Pipilka are the oldest and largest, and own the Hagen Park Motel as well as two coffee plantations; Welyi-Kuta also own two coffee plantations; while Raembka's interests are split between the MP Mr Parua-Kuri and a business rival of his, Mr Goemba-Kot, who founded the Dei Development Company with capital gained from small enterprises mounted under the auspices of the Lutheran mission. Since 1980 Goemba has joined forces with Yap-Roklpa, the young leader who succeeded in being elected as councillor in 1982 for the Kawelka Membo and Mandembo clans. In so doing he has stressed the fact that he is a sister's son of the Mandembo and was in fact brought up on their land at Mbukl, where his father still has his men's house. Together these two have secured influence over the management of a plantation in the Kendipi ward of Dei; have applied for a lease over a large swampy area of land near to the police station and Department of Primary Industry office at Yan; and have, in their guise as representatives of Mend-Want Pty Ltd, a Kawelka-based company, secured a lease on about 140 hectares of land at Ambra. (The Lands Minister granted the Kawelka this as a consolation prize, after refusing to grant them a large piece bordering their own territory at Kuk, which they had been seeking to obtain for many years.)

Gradually, the Hagen countryside is being transformed into areas of capital-intensive high development cash cropping run by business management concerns on behalf of a new élite of national owners, surrounded by areas of less intensively farmed small-holdings occupied by the bulk of the people. Both sectors, however, are fully involved in the cash economy, and the progressive changes in the smallholding sector, though less dramatic and obvious, are no less fundamental than those operating at the 'big business' level. Two points are particularly relevant. First, there has been considerable relocation of settlement, both towards roads when these are newly built and, more strikingly, from high to low-altitude settlement (W. Heaney, undated). The Kawelka's return to their lower-altitude Kuk territory from Mbukl, from 1950 onwards, greatly accelerated in the 1970s as the demand for land for cash crops increased. The land at Mbukl is steep and of variable fertility. At Kuk the drained swampland is dark and rich, and the area, while infested with mosquitoes, is excellent for growing both coffee and traditional *pana* crops, as well as providing rich forage for pigs. Tipuka kinsfolk have joined the Kawelka there and have also gone back to an ancient settlement at Raemb not far from Kuk. Others, along with many Minembi clansmen, have migrated down to the Baiyer around Tigi plantation, where coffee grows fast at an altitude of about 3,000 metres. As the immigrants have expanded in numbers, the groups who originally invited them have either asked them to leave or required payments from them for the use of the land and the right to stay, and the Tipuka have made such payments to the Minembi Andakelkam, their enemies in past warfare, but now their neighbours. As in Pangia, disputes tend to arise when a new development is proposed. In 1982, Kawelka men, utilizing a distant sister's son link, tried to build a club-house for beer drinking in Andakelkam territory, only to meet vigorous opposition from most of the traditional landowners. Later, in 1983, they gained the support of some of the Andakelkam themselves, while others said they would take the matter to court. In the meantime the house was actually opened for the sale of liquor, and business is operating.

The internal balance and rhythm of life has also been fundamentally changed as a result of coffee growing. It is not just, as I have already noted, that *pana* crops are restricted and when grown are often taken to market instead of being consumed. It is also that there are regular shortfalls in sweet potato production in Dei, especially when pig herds are kept at a high level in anticipation of a *moka* festival. Big-men then turn over whole gardens to the pigs. Women do not like this strategy, because they have also to feed their human families. They therefore try to buy sweet potatoes instead, just to feed their pigs. They are then short of this staple, and increasingly during these periods they use coffee money to purchase rice, meat and fish with which to maintain their children. They cannot do this unless the coffee money is available, and it comes only twice, in May and July – August. Hence, and also because this is conveniently during the dry season, the coffee payments determine the timing of *moka* events. By 1982 this was explicitly recognized by big-men. Ndamba of Kawelka Kundmbo told me as much in explaining that a *moka* he planned would be delayed by a further year at least, since the May 1982 coffee harvest was proving unusually thin.

In this chapter I have ranged over a number of issues to do with changing production, coming at last to the point of articulation between production and exchange. Material factors are both constraints and active steering factors in change. Nevertheless, their impact and their own evolution are in a continuous relationship with ideologically-based activities such as *moka* in Hagen and pig kills in Pangia, and it is to these I next turn for more detailed discussion.

Notes

1 J. Burton's extensive ethno-archaeological research in the Aviamp area will shortly provide important insights into how axes were fed into the surrounding Wahgi and Hagen regions.

2 My argument here differs from Watson's argument concerning Pueraria, which he suggested was the original Highlands crop. For him the term *oka* would originally have referred to the Pueraria and so would be ancient. In Melpa this term may in fact be related to the verb 'to dig' (*öki*). See also Watson 1967.

3 The Southern Highlands' Development Authority has had difficulty with its scheme to introduce a group-owned tea plantation near Apenda village in Pangia. People who work on this are prospective owners, but complain that their current part-wages are too low, as if they were in fact only contract workers. They have more than once 'gone on strike' over this.

4 Already in 1967 there were land disputes between these two villages concerning land which abutted on the Station. On one occasion Kauwo men paraded with cordylines (boundary markers) in a protest.

6 Exchange

Exchange is widely recognized as a central preoccupation of men in Highlands societies, and data on it are used by writers of very different theoretical persuasions as a clue to the proper understanding of the dynamics of them, particularly with regard to leadership patterns and the construction of gender. While many introduced institutions and ways of behaving have been taken up, Highlanders have a way of linking these with, or turning them into an occasion for, ceremonial exchange activities. This is pre-eminently true of Hagen, less so in Pangia. In both places, however, exchanges clearly survive even when, for example, pagan cults have been abolished (Pangia) or large business enterprises established (Hagen). In 1965, when I first returned to London from fieldwork in Hagen, I gave a seminar at the School of Oriental and African Studies in which I described the competition for leadership in the *moka*. A student critic argued that this archaic form of competition was purely an artefact of the modern colonial situation and that it would disappear when access to parliamentary democracy was given to the people. I said I thought not, because I saw no reason why both these actiyities could not be pursued when the time came (in fact the first elections had already taken place, in 1964, but people were unfamiliar with their purpose). This was a commonsense reply, but one that was no more grounded in theory than the question itself, which revealed a peculiar juxtaposition of proto-historical materialism and belief in the cultural virtues of the Westminster model of political action. I will now consider the kind of theory needed to understand the circumstances in which ceremonial exchanges flourish or disappear, in situations influenced by colonial rule and post-colonial political change.

C. Gregory (1982) has shown that in fact a correspondence or symbiosis tends to grow between capitalist institutions and indigenous exchange practices. The conditions of correspondence must be looked at from both sides. From the 'capitalist' side, according to Meillassoux's argument, there is an interest in maintaining the coherence of local social systems when these provide the supports to labour migration. In his terms the systems help meet the full costs of reproducing labour power so that the capitalists do not have to do so. If this is correct, it is also true of the institution of the nuclear family in western societies. There is also a doubtful imputed intentionality in the argument; in these terms there may be evidence which suggests quite the contrary, i.e. that certain interests require that local systems be weakened rather than preserved. The removal of labour power itself is bound to have some deleterious effects, as I have noted for Pangia. More specific arguments are needed regarding the economic institutions which are introduced, and more recognition is needed of the fact that indigenous systems themselves may react in accordance with their own logic. Further, it is implausible to relate *all* the ideological concerns of colonial administration simply to the penetration of capitalist enterprise. By the time the Highlands had been opened up, other concerns were evident. It was perceived that it was in Australia's interest to create a stable democratic state to its north. The Australians and Americans had to fight hard to drive out the Japanese during the Second World War, and it was clear that Papua and New Guinea might at any time be taken over by some other Asian power (the 'yellow peril' syndrome). The best way to do this would be to ensure that the two territories coalesced to form a stable, prosperous state dependent on Australian aid and sympathetic to western values, encapsulated in the various Christian missions. Capitalist enterprise has its place in this scheme; it was certainly encouraged rather than tolerated, but one should see it as part of a whole complex of ideas and practices and not attempt to reduce these to a single element. In pursuit of materialist explanations one may point out interesting 'vulgar correlations', such as the fact that the Southern Highlands region was opened up by the kiaps at the time when new labourers were needed to go to the coast, but the Administration as a whole had more than this in mind for the Southern Highlanders. That this is so can be seen simply from the multiplicity of administrative actions. To secure labour it is certainly unnecessary and in fact rather counter-productive to encourage people also to become small-holders or cattle ranchers. But if these policies are seen in the much broader context I have indicated, they make immediate sense. Labour migration is only one phase in the total acculturative process aimed at fashioning a western-style nation.

In this regard exchange practices occupy an uneasy position. They are not 'modern'; they take up time and effort and resources; they show the people in a collective and somewhat independent mood which can be threatening to government authority. At the same time they provide a spectacle for tourists and help promote the image of colonial administration handling an exotic place, and they are also recognized as the most effective means of making peace between warring groups. They give people pride and identity, and help keep the younger generation from becoming 'anti-social'.

It is the issue of resources which occasions most unease. This emerged clearly in debates concerning compensation in the 1970s, when money began to figure more and more extensively in such payments and in *moka*, and ideas of causation were stretched very thin as a justification for demanding cash in compensation payments. University students wrote to the newspapers arguing that only 'traditional' items should be allowed, even as these were disappearing from use in Hagen. The last occasion I saw pearl shells given in Dei was in November–December 1973 when the leader Ndamba used them to pay Kaugel experts for their ritual services in a Female Spirit cult performance. The reasoning was presumably that money should be used for business development and not tied up in ceremonial exchanges. It is a view shared in private by many younger people, and its implication is that the 'traditional' sector of activities should gradually be whittled down by maintaining it in a strictly 'traditional' manner, a kind of indigenous version of the dual economy theory. But this is not how change has operated. As has been pointed out for the Tolai, what is seen as 'traditional' is in fact constantly being modified (Salisbury 1970: 313). In fast-altering contexts the concept of 'tradition' takes on more sharply the character of a legitimizing symbol to which leaders must appeal if they wish to obtain acceptance for their actions. So it is with *moka* in Hagen. Money is legitimized as an instrument for obtaining the status of a leader as it is funnelled into exchanges, and this is in no way seen as being in conflict with the need for such leaders also to be businessmen (A. J. Strathern 1979a). Indeed it is expected that they should have a means of making the money that is spent in this way. At the same time, there is little doubt that the high rates of investment in *moka* do limit the extent to which money is used for other types of investment, for example in house-building or the construction of stores or small factories and workshops. What has happened is that businessmen have used official sources of finance to raise money for activities of this kind, and at the same time have kept money circulating in *moka*. A matter of interest is the extent to which they are able to convert assets from one implicit sphere of operations to another.

This is important, because the pre-contact Highlands systems were founded on rules regarding such conversions which supported the currently dominant categories of people, or else ensured that dominance was held in check. For example, in Hagen there was no direct or regular way of converting foodstuffs into the shell valuables which represented the pinnacle of prestige in *moka*. Foodstuffs had to be fed to the pigs, which could then be exchanged for valuables, even so only within the context of set types of exchange, for which one had to be accepted as an exchange partner. Further, although it was technically possible, say, for a woman to cut a new bush garden or a man to dig sweet potatoes and feed them to his pigs, the conventional division of labour specified clearly that production was a joint responsibility; in this way the division of labour came to be the greatest instrument for maintaining the relations of production.

Why was money taken so readily into exchanges in the Highlands, with their paradoxical combination of innovatory and conservative characteristics? I have looked at this problem elsewhere (A. J. Strathern 1979a), suggesting that a crucial aim of men is to maintain gender hierarchy. When women gained potential access to cash, men found a way to re-appropriate it by defining it as suitable for use in *moka*. The point needs to be argued a little further. Access was obtained through the growing of coffee, and this has a cultural basis in that men recognized with coffee, just as with pigs, that a woman had a claim on what she had helped to produce by direct input of work: in this case the picking and processing of the coffee beans and their transport to the point of sale. Husbands maintained varying practices. Some simply marked out a number of trees and told their wives they could harvest from these for themselves and their children. Some worked with the wife and took the proceeds, dividing them and giving a certain amount (usually less than half) back. But in either case these actions are based on a recognition of women's rights. Money, however, posed a different problem from pigs and shells, which could be funnelled back into the exchange system one way or another, whereas money 'leaks'. Hence the solution of tying it back into *moka*, which women already accepted as legitimate, and indeed of slotting it into the place of shells, which men especially had claimed for themselves in the past. The whole operation had the effect of giving money an ideological anchorage. Using it to purchase vehicles was equally popular at one stage but resulted in more problems. If the vehicle remains, women wish to travel in it. Again, their claims are hard to resist, because their work has helped to purchase it. Ndamba, the Kundmbo leader, placed a twist on this by insisting that only husbands and wives who vigorously took part in *moka* as well as in the purchase of the car could ride in his sub-clan's Toyota truck. This rule was impossible, however, to enforce, since he could not constantly watch over the truck, and his son Nikint was also happy to build his own credit by taking large numbers of extra-clan friends for rides with himself as driver. By 1981 the truck had been redefined as Nikint's own and most of the time it sat in its garage needing repairs and re-licensing, since he was unable to save enough money to put it back on the road without group assistance, and his extra-clan 'friends' had melted away. His 'exploitative' conduct thus resulted in a loss of support, in a manner similar to ways in which such conduct was constrained in the past. Nikint returned to growing coffee and building houses. A third wife, who had joined his other two long-standing spouses when he gained control over the vehicle, left him and the coffee seedlings he had planted far from home at her place became subject to a lengthy court case. By mid-1983 the truck had still not been repaired.

Besides entering *moka* proper, money has become of great importance in bride-wealth payments, and in both Hagen and Pangia the cash component of these has risen considerably in recent years, just as in Hagen during the 1950s, the shell component rose enormously from just a few to as many as fifty. One of the first actions of the Local Government Council in Dei was to place a limit on the size of bride-wealth payments, decreeing that for a previously unmarried girl these should be twenty shells and ten pigs, and for a divorced or widowed women half this or less. As far as I am able to tell, this rule was not one of those instigated by the kiaps, but was consistent with their view that exchanges should not become too 'inflated'. The amounts actually paid nearly always exceeded these specified limits, and I know of no case in which anyone laid a complaint to this effect before the Council. However, perhaps the limit did keep payments down somewhat. From the mid-1970s onwards the rule has not been referred to at all. Originally, an additional £100 was specified as the maximum amount of money, but this too was very soon exceeded, and by 1982 amounts of K2,000 were demanded and, in a few cases, given. High as they seem, two factors must be kept in mind in evaluating them. One is that as the supply of a particular valuable increases, while the 'supply' of brides in relation to the number of grooms remains the same, it is inevitable that a balancing mechanism will be found. The second is that a certain amount of extra pressure is fed back into the system by the practice of polygamy. This increases the scarcity of brides and therefore forces the rates of payment up. My use of market terminology here should not be taken as suggesting that a simple market situation holds here, nor that bride-wealth is a market transaction. It is rather the foundation of an expected alliance, the more a family receives the more it is expected to give back in return gifts. Even so, questions of supply and demand are not irrelevant, since the system of exchange cannot exist in isolation from such factors as the availability of valuables and the demographic reproduction of the population.

Why, then, was it necessary for the Council to limit the payments, if they could be expected to achieve their own equilibrium? The processes of feedback which would lead to equilibrium were far from perfect, since they operated through the domestic level, without any political regulation. A family with many daughters and few sons stood to gain, whereas one with the reverse would be hard-pressed, even if aid could be requested from the wider lineage group. Further a family which had a good supply of pigs and valuables, for whatever reason, might set a high level of payment for its daughters, and this would be met only by families of similar standing. Implicitly, a kind of stratification in marriage would emerge, analogous to a system of social class. The Council regulation would thus restrict the development of such inequality, although this was not the reason given at the time. The fact that the Council no longer seriously attempts to regulate bride-wealth might mean either that the problem has disappeared or that social inequality and the emergence of classes is now further advanced. I think that the latter is closer to the truth. The pressure of polygamy may have been reduced somewhat by the fact that most people are now baptized in the Lutheran church, which absolutely forbids plural marriage. But the desire of parents to contract valuable alliances has increased, and this is certainly true also of baptized Lutherans, who often have a strong sense of doing 'business', imported by the mission itself. Furthermore, the idea of polygamy is so strong that baptized church members sometimes lapse, and other people have simply stayed outside the church because they are already polygamists; their children follow suit. It is also the case that families sometimes deliberately marry a beautiful young woman to an older man and then encourage her to break the marriage. In one such instance the man was already married to a wife with four children. When he married his second wife the first one left and took her children with her. He paid K2,000 and a Toyota Stout vehicle for the new wife, who bore him a son. Later she secretly killed her child and after a brief period of mourning went back to her own kin, prepared to marry a younger husband for more bride-wealth. The evidence here is all hearsay, but it falls into the pattern. I do not think the pattern is entirely new, but this kind of manoeuvering has probably been intensified by the advent of cash. In the case of pigs the potentialities are rather different. No technology has been introduced to ease the labour of rearing them: one does not find many small piggeries set up to raise them for market in parallel with the small-holdings of coffee, nor has the Department of Primary Industry attempted to set these up. A few were established in connection with the tea blocks which were set up in the 1960s in conjunction with a large tea estate in the Wahgi Valley. People on the resettlement blocks at Kindeng and Kondapena in the Wahgi, mostly from the Enga area, also run such piggeries. These people are more oviously 'peasants' than those living on customary land claims, but they and the others are bound together in a single economic complex.[1] The work of raising pigs is laborious and continuous, and there is always the risk of loss by theft or sickness. If men are away, women are expected to carry out all the tasks of caring for the herd other than twisting the fibres to make tethering ropes. So the work itself is a major factor in controlling what women do, and a woman whose pigs multiply receives lavish praise from men. Conversely, a woman whose pigs suffer from worms and are emaciated will be condemned by both sexes. Along with the stability of pig production goes a comparable stability in their exchange use. Their supply cannot be easily increased beyond a certain level, although it can always, of course, drop if women refuse to do the necessary work. By contrast, the potential for unequal accumulation of assets which transactions based on cash bring with them is much greater.

While the production of coffee has, up to the late 1970s, expanded, and the acquisition of new areas of land for development has become the chief economic 'game' played, the production and use of pigs has remained relatively stable in both Pangia and Hagen since the 1960s. The only alterations which have occurred have been the progressive introduction of new cross-bred stock into the Pangia pig population, the practice of buying large pigs to use as prestige items for exchange in Hagen and the occasional marketing of pork in both places. This continuing emphasis on pigs, no matter what the status of other valuables, is firmly grounded in female labour. When in his 1974 *moka* speech Ongka declared that he was doubtful if there would be another similar big *moka*, his explanation was that 'the young women do not work as the women of old used to; they are too interested in keeping themselves washed and pretty' (A. J. Strathern 1979b: 121). It is true that girls wash and decorate themselves whenever they go to market or town, and also that they use every opportunity to do so. But on marriage this changes. Unless a girl moves out through education and/or marriage to an outsider, she inherits the full range of women's tasks at the time she goes to her husband's place, and women's pride is much bound up with their pig herds. Pigs are therefore important to them, though their evaluations may differ from those of the men. By contrast the valuation of shells and cash has altered markedly over time. Arguably, rates of exchange have been aimed at adjusting them to the indigenous 'pig standard'. A semi-grown local pig in 1982 in Dei was worth K300 and a large one K600 to K800. With ten pigs, a notional number for bride-wealth in the case of a first marriage, it is clear that in cash terms marriage payments were worth at least K5,000. This is close to the full cash amount in Motu bride-wealths as paid during the 1970s in the long-urbanized Hanuabada village near Port Moresby on the Papuan coast. As I noted earlier, live pigs fetch much more than when sold as cooked pork, and bride-wealth payments *must* include such pigs. If a groom had to obtain them all by cash purchase, marriage would indeed be beyond most people's means. As it is, grooms have to depend on their kin network. In Pangia, this fact was a major lever in inducing young men to distribute their cash earnings from work on coastal plantations. In one case in 1967 a youth protested that he would not divide his cash, but his senior kin determinedly went ahead and prepared pigs for his bride-wealth. Two days after he returned to the village he opened his box and gave away almost all he had brought with him, and the next day his bride-wealth was paid.

At no time in Hagen has the use of land for coffee proceeded to the extent that it did earlier in central Chimbu (Brookfield 1973). There, little pasture was left for pigs, and economic issues were sharply posed: pigs would have to be given up, or penned up, or coffee areas abandoned, or vegetable gardens not made. The reason for the swiftly emergent crisis was simply population pressure. In such heavily-populated areas in the past warfare may well have played a particularly important role in decimating or dispersing groups. Then if later mission influence was strong, the religious supports for the taboo on sexual intercourse fell away, allowing population numbers to climb steeply. All Highlands societies appear to have had a taboo of this kind, quite explicitly connected with the health of the child rather than with the welfare of the mother or the need to avoid over-population. Indeed, men give it as a reason for polygyny: because of the taboo they must have more wives in order to have more children! Nevertheless, it must have acted as an overall brake on demographic growth. One can understand why the missions have advocated the relaxation of the rule. Since they forbid polygyny but are not in a position to urge the restriction of intercourse or the reduction of family numbers, they are bound to allow a closer spacing of children than is traditionally approved. In the densely-populated Highlands valleys and mountains this is certainly an unfortunate change, and one which cannot be fully counterbalanced by the advice of the health clinics run as a service by the mission, to the effect that young children must be fed with mashed vegetable food as well as breast milk prior to weaning.

Since the pig economy has never really been threatened by a serious crisis, it remains the backbone of exchanges in both areas. Live pig *moka* and pig killing festivals have continued since the 1960s with no sharp break or any lengthening of the periods between them. Indeed, since 1978 these festivals have taken on a revived and expansive appearance in Pangia, paralleling their 1960s boom in Hagen. The 'revival', minor as it is, has three components: first, the full resumption of decorations, with face paint designs and feather head-dresses, which were frowned on by the missions at Tunda in the 1960s; second, the resumption of certain categories of gifts, notably the prestige-bringing *kange* payments, in which big-men solicit contributions of pearl shells from lineage kin and others and then pay these to the maternal kin of a deceased relative, or else for themselves, in anticipation of their eventual death; and third in the practice of building special longhouses of the kind described in Chapter 3. What is of sociological interest in this cultural revival is that it coincides with the end of the kiap era in Pangia, and suggests that once this form of authoritarian rule faded away the people felt more at ease in following their own customs. What the kiaps achieved in Pangia was a sudden concentration of power in themselves in a society in which power had previously been highly dispersed. During their time of dominance certain 'successor' roles were fostered which acquired part of this power. These were the positions of councillor and Village Court magistrates, the latter in fact coming into operation only after most of the expatriate kiaps had left. But these are only pale reflections of the autocratic power once exercised by the patrolling kiap and his police. As a result, local groups now feel more able to express their political rivalries and hostilities, which were distinctly muted in the 1960s. The chief ways in which this is done are by cutting and presenting pork in a certain way, and by arranging the lines of decorated men who enter a pig killing ground in such a way that the men at the front are those whose fathers killed or were killed by the donors in past warfare, or by sorcery.

In 1967 warfare was only eight years distant, and yet discussion of it was distinctly muted in the Pangia men's houses; nor was it 'preserved' in ceremonial speeches as is done in Hagen. It was, as I have said, as though the past had been suspended, if not abolished. My questions about it eventually produced the descriptions of 'madness' that followed shortly after pacification, and accounts of this were listened to with uproarious laughter. The madness marked the huge transition between 'then' and 'now'. But gradually the past is being retrieved and reconstituted as it is in Hagen *moka* exchanges. In these the explicit blending of past and present is done in speeches. In Pangia it is done in the arrangement of pork gifts themselves, particularly by loading recipients with large numbers of heavy legs of pork and of presenting whole or half-carcasses cut through the middle rather than separating the legs (skin) from the insides (rib-cage). In both cases the pork is thereby made 'heavy', and if the recipients stumble in carrying it off they are expected to become sick or die. The donors also swing their clubs when the recipients march in, and when killing the pigs they say '*Ne te moa*', 'You get faeces'. I observed this in the remote village of Lawe at a pig kill in 1967 when the Lawe people entertained their ex-enemies of Wembu; the reference is directly to their enemies with whom the pig is identified. In giving the dead pig to the recipient, the donors are giving death. The same principle of metaphorical identification of people with objects, to which I referred in Chapter 2, holds here. This identification may either be with oneself or one's recipient; here it is with the recipient. In the 'proper', separated-out forms of giving, the rib-cage of the pig is removed and it is given by wife-givers back to wife-takers as a kind of 'body', like the body of the wife who was given or the body of the sister's children themselves. The wife-takers give shells, durable wealth, representing here the maleness of their 'name'. Each side in a sense gives itself; but the rib-cage stands both for those who give it and those for whom it is given.

The symbolic operation of exchange in Pangia thus consists of an endless cycle of self-giving which entails also an identification of donor with recipient. The hostile gift, *poi mokora*, however, breaks sharply away from this identification, and it is interesting to note that it has two modalities, one of which we might call 'classic Wiru' practice, and one which resembles Hagen custom. The first is *poi mokora* proper in which a whole pig is given but is sliced in two in the middle. The symbolism here is definitely metaphorical. The second is the presentation of numerous legs or whole sides, slapped down in front of the recipients. Although the metaphorical character of the pig is still present (*kai one tele tanea*, 'the pig is a strong thing', is the phrase used), it is also used here metonymously: many different parts of pigs add up to a massive 'weight' (see Sillitoe 1981).

In Hagen, too, when pork legs are given the aim is to make them weighty, but the arrangement is rather different. One of the donors first calls to a recipient as representative of his group to come forward and stand before him. The other donors approach and slap pork legs and other pieces on his shoulder. He must hold them firmly and not drop any as he takes them back to his people, otherwise this is an omen that a group member will die. The logic here is similar to that in Pangia, but there is no idea that in this context the act of giving is itself hostile and aimed at causing such a slip to be made.

The other symbolic element to which I referred is the choice of who should head the line of recipients as they march to their station in the pig-kill ground. There is no dancing as such. The men walk in stiffly, each muscle and feather on rigid display, and their enemies as well as their friends size up their physical condition as well as the splendour and correctness of their decorations. Hunched shoulders or wrinkled skin are taken as signs that their bearer already suffers from some 'weight' (*kenda*), and is vulnerable. The man who goes first is at chief risk. He shows his male 'face' to all and must carry himself well. The line may be directed to walk over uneven or slippery ground in expectation that one of their number will trip. When the men of Pupi village came into Mamuane in 1980 at the stage of presenting lengths of sugarcane, the man who walked first in this way was the son of someone who had killed a Mamuane recipient by a *poi mokora* gift on an earlier occasion. He was risking his life to uphold the prestige of his father, and his presence was a challenge to the Mamuane men, who had themselves built their longhouse *Dapanda* as a challenge to the Tunda-Pupi axis of allies.

These aspects of pig kills were not well known to me in 1967, but they are much more strongly articulated now than they were at the height of the kiap-cum-mission regime. It is hard to tell whether they are in a sense new elements or if they are simply revivals of pre-colonial custom. It is not impossible for actions to be both these things, but in this instance I think that they are a straight revival. The time-depth is not great. We are dealing with a twenty-year period between first pacification and 1983, and this period is comparable to that which had elapsed in Dei Council between pacification and my first fieldwork there in 1964, the Dei area not being closely administered until towards the end of the Second World War. It is also equivalent to a short generation, and may be understood as the period it takes for a people to adjust to dramatic new changes and pressures in their lives. Elsewhere, in the Highlands fringes, there is evidence that mission impact was highly traumatic and caused the people at first entirely to alter certain aspects of their life style, for example their dwelling houses. The typecase here is the Karimui area, as described by Wagner (1974). Later, they return more to their previous normal pattern, if allowed to do so.

But such revived practices also exist in a changed overall context. This was very clear in a pig kill observed at Mele village, an Evangelical Bible Mission stronghold, in 1978. A mission group insisted on holding a hymn and prayer session in the middle of the ceremonial ground, followed by a harangue, before distribution could begin. Further, the donors included a large amount of store-bought food in their gifts: large quantities of cooked rice and tins of fish were heaped up before the decorated recipients. In some cases whole boxes of fish and bags of rice were stacked up in imitation of the traditional *poi mokora* action. But clearly this was an innovation, and one which was most marked around Pangia Station, where access to cash and store goods was greatest. In 1967 I had attended a cooking of rice and fish at Mamuane village, held for the baptism of several people into the Lutheran church. Similar cookings are held in Hagen to mark the end of the first phase of mourning at a funeral, and also to celebrate baptisms, although at these pigs are usually killed. The common feature in these examples is that in all instances there is an important exchange element. Christian baptisms would simply not be complete without an elaborate cooking of food. Those who receive should make their return when they or others of their village are baptized, so that a new exchange cycle emerges based on the round of baptisms in an area. New elements accrete also to *moka* occasions. For example, at a money *moka* in 1980 held by the Kawelka Kundmbo, young men also held a 'coming out' party for one of their number who had been extremely sick and was said to have been 'poisoned' (sorcerized) by enemies. The men wore decorations that combined traditional elements with bright tinsel paper, and some of them played bamboo pipes as a band, wearing the obligatory dark glasses. They drew an interested knot of spectators, mostly women, who in no way interfered with or replaced the main event.

Similar 'parties' are held in town, especially by Hagen people who are living with their families. When men receive their fortnightly pay, they like to buy a number of chickens and steam-cook these with vegetables, finishing off the party with as much beer as they can afford (or more, since if they can, they 'borrow' more money from tipsy friends and buy black market beer at double the store price). This practice ensures a kind of 'consumption' return for both sexes at the time when money comes in from wages. Over half the fortnight's income often goes in such a party, followed by an intensive and long-lasting game of cards, played for money stakes, which may last until the Monday morning. Women continue the game throughout the week if they have the money to do so. There is little doubt that Hagen women in town are prone to become heavy gamblers, much more so than are women from Pangia, and there is also little doubt that this is because the principles of *moka* exchange themselves encourage a risk-taking and profit-seeking approach. Women have been allowed more easily into playing cards than into *moka*, however, since cards are condemned by big-men as basically 'rubbish' by comparison with *moka* itself, and so there is not such great resistance to women's participation. In both areas cards were a great preoccupation during the 1960s. Playing cards for money was oficially banned, and the kiaps regularly sought out and prosecuted players in Pangia, while in Hagen attitudes tended to be more lax. Councillors used the issue as a pretext to report youths as they did, for example, in the case of failure to turn up for roadwork. In both areas, too, there was a constant search for magical aids to assist one in winning, and cards magic was simply called 'win'. I was frequently and earnestly requested to bring some from London or Hong Kong or wherever its true source was, just as I was also asked to bring scent (*wel-santa*) which was assumed to be a form of direct love potion (*amb kopna*, *aroa mi*, in the Melpa and Wiru languages). Card games were definitely most attractive when they were were illicit and actively discouraged by kiaps (the same being true of the Wape of West Sepik as described by Mitchell 1978). They are also continuous omen-takings at which one's luck, or supernatural support, is proved or disproved; as such they represent a kind of speeded-up version of *moka* itself. Outcomes occur or are reversed over periods of minutes, hours, and days rather than weeks, months, and years as in the actual *moka*, and one wrests money automatically from an opponent rather than receiving it as a gift. At a certain period in Hagen, playing cards was also undoubtedly a young men's game, engaged in as a statement of difference from the older generation. The older men responded, however, by taking an interest in the outcomes of games, by encouraging *moka* based on initial card games, and by saying in their speeches that they were giving *moka* so that relations between groups would remain friendly and card games would be safe to play. Gradually, therefore, such games were brought into the ordinary pattern of activities, and they still continue. In Pangia, the response was different; there councillors and magistrates prosecute players whenever they find them, while surreptitiously playing themselves. The games therefore continue to be illicit and a focus for younger men returned from working elsewhere.

The final context in which I wish to look at exchange is one I have touched on earlier: the introduced political arena. It is particularly evident that in Dei the long-standing success of the MP, Mr Parua-Kuri, has more to do with his achieved place in traditional politics than with his United Party membership or his performance in the Parliament itself. His own claim that so long as he has been Member the area has not had problems of tribal conflict may be read in another way: as a threat that if he should ever fail to be re-elected his supporters would make trouble. I am not suggesting that this is what he meant, but events following the 1982 elections do suggest that violence is now becoming established as a response to political losses in this arena.

Overall, the MP is definitely seen as in an exchange relationship with his electors, and from the first the problem has been to know how this relationship is to be constituted. The formal conception of the MP's role has been that of the mediator who can secure projects for his area from the Parliament. Not all MPs can do this, however, and in practice what counts much more for the individual voter is what the MP can do for him. A way of surmounting this problem was found by the Sir Julius Chan-Mr Iambakey Okuk coalition in 1981. MPs were given funds from the sectoral programmes for provincial development, and were empowered to bypass Provincial Governments in presenting these directly to the people, as they chose. This was quite against the spirit in which the Provincial Governments had been set up and was a sure recipe for criticism, if not corruption. But it did achieve its aim, and in cases where the MP spread his money widely it paid off in re-election during 1982, whereas many other MPs lost their seats. Once re-elected these men were likely to survive any attempts to unseat them. In Pangia, Mr Pundia Kange also maintained his position by consistent generosity at a domestic level, and there is no doubt that this had an impact. He had the resources to do so, and sitting MPs have to behave like redistributive 'chiefs' and not just big-men. In Dei, however, Parua's strength was assured by his existing exchange ties in *moka* proper and by his mastery of traditional rhetoric. In this respect, he had himself become something of a symbol for Dei electorate itself, not unconnected with his wounding and disfigurement by a Mul Council attacker more than a decade before 1982. His position was doubly strong, both because of this special status, and because he was also a traditional-style big man. The fact that he may, like others, have distributed sectoral programme money as he saw fit was minor by comparison. The challenge to him from younger men therefore failed. He was also, according to some, responsible for encouraging weak rivals to stand against him simply in order to split the votes of stronger ones, and it was even alleged that he paid for people's nomination fees to achieve this end. I have no knowledge as to whether this is true, but as an allegation it is significant. People *assume* that such manoeuvres are being made by politicians in order to secure the personal 'line of power' for themselves, and are concerned only to the extent that they themselves can gain something, as it were, at a point along that line, much as they attempted to do, by different means, in the money cult of 1968–71 which flourished most extensively in Dei. The chief historical significance of this cult is as an experiment which failed in its object of 'producing' money directly, but at the same time completed the transition in the economy away from pearl shells and towards dependence on money itself (A. J. Strathern 1979–80).

Three factors work together, then, in supporting the position of MPs. One is the overall segmented structure of social groupings, in which leaders are 'enclaved'; the second is the fact that as ordinary MPs they cannot always obtain definite projects for their areas. This is the source of their conflict with Provincial Government members, and the reason why they were given sectoral funds to bypass the latter in the pre-national election year. The third is at a deep cultural level: the 'exchange model' of social relations which actors have, a model which enables them to tolerate inequality provided there is some definite reciprocity. It is in this spirit that at the time of elections prominent supporters claim their candidate's vehicle as their own, to take them home after meetings or for whatever purpose; after the elections these exchanges usually are allowed by the MP to drop to a lower level of intensity. This collocation of factors shows the structure we have become accustomed to in the preceding pages: material constraints and opportunities plus cultural ideas. While they obviously cohere in specific event-complexes it remains hard, if not impossible, to apply linear models of causation to them. In Chapter 7 I shall review a small selection of the literature on social change in Melanesia in the light of what this narrow investigation of Hagen and Pangia has suggested.

Note

1 Further Enga settlers have moved into the territories of Hagen groups on the basis of friendship, as men from Tomba have come to Kuk.

7 Explanations

'Explanation' has itself been an elusive concept in social anthropology (R. Brown 1973). It is what we all seek, since 'explanation' is seen as the best kind of 'understanding'. Explanation is also seen as the discovery of causes, and where causation is clearly multiple the strain of looking for single final determinants becomes great. Social situations do not present themselves in experimental but in phenomenological guises, and attempts to force them into experimental strait-jackets, whether by statistical or structural analysis, have remained incomplete. Nevertheless, the attempt must be made if we are to move beyond the descriptive level, and the only pragmatic way to begin is by using a combination of structural analysis and comparative ethnography. I have done this in relation to two population areas in a much wider region, chiefly because I have worked in these areas myself, and can therefore provide a fairly comprehensive context in which to set the comparison. Such a method has its limits, and one cannot argue from it that wider trends in Papua New Guinea are to be inferred; rather, the reverse is true. These wider trends must also be known in order to make full sense of local events and responses to change. I have brought wider matters to bear when these have been clearly relevant, but it cannot be claimed that the result is a comprehensive picture. Instead, my concern has been, in a sense, technical, and focused on two issues: first, what differences between the selected areas emerge from social structure, exchange, and the cultural notions which go with these practices? Second, when we combine the results of such an approach with a consideration of twenty years of history, particularly political and economic changes, what role can strictly 'material' factors be said to play in these changes? My conclusion has been that conceptually material and cultural factors can indeed be distinguished, but that the question of dominance or determination between them cannot be settled. The results then, are ethnographic rather than 'scientific' and 'universal'. But they certainly provide pointers for similar understandings of processes elsewhere in the Highlands and Melanesia.

In this chapter, then, I consider three other works more or less explicitly dealing with the analysis of change in this region. These are: R. F. Salisbury's *From Stone to Steel*, first published in 1962; P. Brown's *Highlands Peoples of New Guinea* (1978); and *Persistence and Exchange*, edited by R. W. Force and P. Bishop (1981). The studies are chosen because their authors show a concern for factors labelled as 'economic', and these have been a starting point for the problems which I have discussed here. My aim is not to make a comprehensive review, but rather to probe the arguments which have so far been adduced.

Salisbury's early account remains of outstanding interest and value, although from certain viewpoints it uneasily attempts to combine 'substantivist' and 'formalist' approaches to the Siane economy. In fact, some such combination has to be attempted if we are to achieve both 'cultural' and 'sociological' analysis. Salisbury does this by looking on the one hand at the indigenous classification of goods and how these are structured in spheres of exchange, and on the other at the allocation of time and other resources to activities, including production and ceremonial exchange. One of his early points on change is similar to that which I have made for Hagen: the European's practice of exchanging shell valuables directly for vegetables broke the rules of exchange (or, in my reformulation, it bypassed the relations of production). Salisbury adds a useful cultural observation: the newcomers' behaviour was peculiar to the Siane and could be explained only on the basis that they were spirits who had 'seemingly inexhaustible stores of valuables' and were willing to give them away for 'things of no account' such as food (p. 114). The same point explains why the people also thought that all objects connected with these strange intruders would change into shells if flutes were blown and pigs sacrificed over them. When this failed to happen, Salisbury says, they 'now realized that the visitors were men and not spirits'. One may wonder a little about this, since in both Hagen and Pangia the idea that Europeans may be spirits continues to be entertained along with the normal working assumption that they are probably people. Salisbury's second point (p. 116) is that the creation of patrol posts from which steel axes and shells were disbursed tended to create an imbalance in the relative accumulation of women in marriage, until outlying areas were actually short of women and pigs (pp. 116–17). If this is true, and it seems likely enough, it is also the case that such imbalances may have formed a part of the pre-contact patterns of distribution. Centres of pig production should have been able to pull in more shell valuables and also women if their men so wished. Over a range of some forty miles in the Mt Hagen region, at any rate, it is evident that while in the Central Ogelbeng plain large tribal groups and numbers of multiple polygynists were common, in Tambul, at a high altitude and away from the trade routes in shells, there was a high proportion of permanent bachelors. Salisbury points out that higher rates of payment would gradually cause a new balance to spread through the population, but it is also likely that some more long-lasting inequalities were generated at this time. He himself notes that the power of big-men increased once all valuables passed into the nexus of activities which they dominated; whereas I have argued for Hagen that initially the influx of valuables must have meant a certain 'democratization' of the competition for big-manship.

Salisbury's most well-known point, widely quoted and subsequently re-tested by Godelier and Garanger (1973), Townsend (1969), and Sillitoe (1979), is that the new steel axes enabled a saving in time on subsistence activities, and therefore freed men first for more fighting and after pacification for more exchange. Here the 'and therefore' needs to be evaluated with care. These events were not an automatic result of the introduction of steel, and their impact was mediated entirely through the existing cultural and social structure. So indeed were the forms of manipulation which emerged, for example when Siane men closer to the government station traded leather belts for other, traditional, luxuries, with outlying groups. Their partners still thought of the belts as 'valuables', and 'their joy in receiving them was joy at being given valuables for luxuries' (p. 121). Reclassification, like higher rates of exchange, would gradually have spread outwards. If the argument is correct, it should apply to all Highlands centres where government stations were set up. I have earlier employed an argument regarding imbalance to explain the Nebilye valley shell cult of the 1940s. When Salisbury's fieldwork was done in 1952, it was only seven years after Siane *bosbois* had called in Administration patrols to halt the fighting which resulted from blood feuds following a dysentery epidemic. (This epidemic went right through to the Western Highlands about this time, causing widespread deaths, and was interpreted as being caused by sorcery. Influenza and dysentry hit Pangia later, around 1960, when the Station was set up and policemen from coastal places brought in.)

In terms of production, Salisbury notes that returning contract labourers brought a wide range of new goods with them and were required to distribute these; however, most of these were for consumption rather than tools to increase production. His whole study was done before coffee seedlings were introduced, and in order to follow the picture of change in the Eastern Highlands one has to switch from the Siane to Goroka further to the east, where Finney (1973) described the enthusiastic adoption of this new cash crop and the rapid demise of pearl shells by comparison with cash. Salisbury's study therefore acquires an archaic character, being concerned with only the first of the two major changes at the technological and productive level in Highlands societies. How would he have handled the question of coffee within his own framework? No doubt he would have analysed the progressive tendency to allocate more time and work to coffee growing and selling, and then gone on to examine whether big-men were able to increase their power as effectively by means of coffee as they had done earlier through shell valuables. This would depend on the constraints involved. With valuables, all that was required was that they should enter the ceremonial nexus and that big-men still controlled this. With money, however, the situation is more complicated, since it has a large variety of uses and can be earned by both sexes. This is why the use of money has brought to the fore the question of gender relations in Highlands societies.

In his final synthesis Salisbury repeats the argument that the introduction of steel tools was not at first used to produce more subsistence goods, but instead the time was employed in struggles for power. Two points are relevant here. First, it was men's time rather than women's which was set free. Siane women were not allowed in any case to use axes.

Their tool, the digging stick, remained as it was, and men certainly did not use their extra time to take on women's tasks. Second, the increased ceremonial activities were no doubt based mostly on a stepped-up velocity of circulation, but it is likely that over time the pressure on women to rear more pigs would be increased. Further, women would be involved in taking pigs from place to place, so their effective gardening time would also be reduced.

Salisbury then proceeds to elaborate a general model of change in Siane society. He begins by supposing the society to have been in equilibrium, but this, I would suggest, is an unnecessary assumption. Technological change then produced a greater struggle for power through prestige tokens, he says, and this ended in greater political centralization. Further increases in wealth were then used to provide luxuries and raise the standard of living. Problems emerge if outsiders 'retain ownership of the capital investments and enable the natives to obtain luxuries without making investments'. Problems also emerge when money enters the system. Bohannon's study of the Nigerian Tiv, cited by Salisbury, shows this clearly. The Tiv used subsistence goods to procure valuables which they then employed in bride-wealth so that as they struggled to become more wealthy in people 'they are merely selling more and more of their foodstuffs and subsistence goods, leaving less and less for their own consumption' (p. 211). Alternatively, people may hoard their money and not re-invest, which causes the economy to stagnate, as Belshaw argued it did in Southern Massim societies in Papua (p. 212).

This is a descriptive model, which states what people have done in a number of cases and suggests that therefore they may do so more widely. The African citation is particularly interesting here, as it shows that these processes of change are by no means confined to Melanesia. It would be worthwhile examining the African literature in more detail, armed with this 'Melanesian model'. Restating the description more sharply, one may say that the *reason why* change proceeds in this way is because of the existing domination of categories of leaders (chiefs, big-men, elders). Further, one must recognize that these leaders were also often reconstituted by the colonial power, and in the early stages of contact some had become 'satraps', as Paula Brown has said. It is also true that both pre and post-contact these same social systems might throw up temporary despotic characters, as Salisbury and others have argued elsewhere (Salisbury 1964; Brown 1963; Watson 1971). Unless these consolidate themselves at the productive level, however, their power is strictly temporary. The stage referred to by Salisbury as a kind of blockage in investment was reached very quickly in the Highlands, and has now been transcended by the rapid entry of certain people into large-scale capital investment via business development corporations, and facilitated by the presence of university-trained manpower. The potential for inequality between the owning and managerial élite and the ordinary people has thus increased enormously, and a class society is in the process of being created. Investment of money produces more riches for some, while the strain of maintaining both a subsistence and a ceremonial sector contributes to the gradual 'peasantization' of the masses. The social processes thus appear general, but rest also on certain cultural responses, and are in no way automatic consequences of material changes.[1]

I will now turn to Paula Brown's study of the Highlands region. She stresses the role of ecology, agricultural practices, and population densities to a greater extent than Salisbury, who is more interested in exchange. Brown's book is very valuable as an overall survey, and her theoretical point of departure, although anodyne, is unexceptionable: 'There is an ecological system of organisms in an environment, a cultural system of beliefs and practices, and a social system of relationships and groups. . . . My account attempts to show how these systems are interdependent' (p. 1). Social change is recognized throughout the work, but is focused with difficulty, because the arrangement of topics as a whole is synchronic. Here, I shall examine only Chapter 2, on agriculture and population. It argues that four areas in the Highlands have become 'centres of agricultural development and population growth' (p. 66). The concept Brown employs is that of 'agricultural intensification', either in terms of 'the relationship in the time of cultivation and fallow' (as Boserup) or 'the techniques and labour input at various stages of gardening' (p. 76). These may include enclosures, type of fallow encouraged, tillage, erosion control, water control, fertilization, and crop care, including weeding.

She finds that the most intensive agriculture, by a combination of these criteria, was found in only four areas, Kapauku, Dani, Enga, and Chimbu, each with 'less populous areas around a closely settled and continuously occupied core' (p. 99). She suggests that a density of 125 people per square mile may be the limit for shifting, long-fallow cultivation practices. Above that, a more permanent settlement pattern emerges. At more moderate densities one may find smaller cores with other areas cultivated and occupied intermittently.

A number of points may be made here. The first is that this is a potential basis for studying pre-contact change. The four areas can only have *evolved* into their state at the time of contact through population growth. Highlands peoples themselves speak of change in these terms: a group starts with one founder, grows big, and its branches move out from a centre. Hence a population centre may be an area from which people have dispersed as population increased, resulting in internecine conflict and the dislodging of some groups; the history of groups in the Wahgi area suggests a pattern of this kind. Then, it may generally be supposed that institutions of exchange *both* are used as a means of stabilizing social relations in areas of high density *and* themselves produce further strains resulting from the intensive competition of individual big-men. In addition, once one enters the colonial period, the causes of centralization of population alter. Roads and stations are built, and these become points of dispersal for new goods. Entrepreneurs, in particular, are attracted to placing their houses, trade-stores, coffee pulping machines, and gardens near roads. The Administration may also order people to live together in villages or build individual houses rather than communal longhouses set in the bush. This is an especially important point for Pangia. There the people were told to build villages as a consolidation of their hamlets. There is some confusion as to the result. Government officials say this was not an explicit directive but more of a spontaneous innovation. Nor was it entirely new: for pig killings people also build communal villages. The longer they stayed in them the further they had to walk to their gardens and the more intense became political factionalism. The result, on both grounds, was a re-dispersal into smaller local groups.

By careful comparison of systems and the use of statistical tests, Brown concludes that land tenure practices are also an outcome of population density and agricultural intensification working together. Thus 'individual land tenure is a product of short fallow and frequent land use' (p. 111), the pattern which had developed in central Chimbu. Here, then, there is a definite indication that a cultural practice is the precipitate of certain material factors, but these are never found out of association with further social and cultural variables, particularly the development of big-manship and ceremonial exchange.

From the point of view of the present study, Brown's discussions are interesting but not crucial, other than in the sense that in terms of intensification, the Hagen area is clearly developed more than Pangia; this is certainly reflected in the form of the exchange systems in the two areas.

Pangia is literally on the edge of the classic Highlands form of adaptation. Southwards, in Erave, one enters the Highlands fringe, where agriculture is much less intensive and densities are lower. The big-man system disappears, and is replaced by prominent mediums who appear to have a political as well as a religious role.

The last set of studies I shall consider, Force and Bishop's, returns us to the realm of exchange theory. *Persistence and Exchange* has as its focus the Pacific region as a whole. In Pacific Island societies the process of incorporation into the world economic system is more generally advanced than it is in the Highlands of Papua New Guinea. Yet in this region also one finds that pre-capitalist structures of exchange and feasting continue. The 'trade' aspects of such exchanges disappear, as in the case of the *Motu Hiri* expedition, the Huon Gulf trade system, the Trobriands *kula*, and the movement of *moka* between the Hagen and Enga regions, which facilitated the transfer of stone axes from Hagen and ash-salt from Enga. What is retained is the prestige-seeking element, in which gender relations are usually implicated. There is no problem in changing the types of goods involved so that the exchange system has a point of articulation with the introduced capitalist economy. Foodstuffs purchased with money or money itself are funnelled into exchanges, as in the Highlands, and the system therefore becomes dependent on the wider economic structure for its own reproduction. This was already true, as Harding notes (p. 145), albeit on a smaller-scale, in the pre-contact systems.

Those accounts which stress persistence as such usually take on a functionalist cast. This does not mean that on this ground alone they are to be rejected. In ethnographic terms, for example, Fischer's (Force and Bishop: Chapter 6) study of feasts in Ponape of the Caroline Islands is convincing. He lists as the societal functions of feasting the exchange of special local resources (e.g. seafoods as against coconuts and breadfruits), these foods still being desired and valuable and trade continuing as it does, for instance, between Ialibu and Pangia in the Highlands for the exchange of high-altitude nut pandanus with low-altitude fruit pandanus, and in Dei Council between Dei and the Jimi valley in terms of the exchange of winged beans for pandanus fruit. There is redistribution of temporary surpluses, stimulation of production as emergency reserve, compensation for the political leadership of chiefs, old age security, and an orderly outlet for competition. In terms of individual motivation, he cites the assurance of land rights and the quest for prestige and titles. There are indications that Salisbury's model might apply here, since Fischer notes that with the introduction into feasts of purchased foods, some kinds of feasts 'especially funeral feasts and title payment feasts' are becoming larger. In general, we must search for the conditions of reproduction, expansion, or attrition of these systems. In this instance there is probably a parallel with the potlatch, at which titles were also gained. Fischer tells us that the competition for titles is now more open: linkage to the external political and economic system has weakened the principle of hereditary succession by chiefs.

Only one of the longer papers in Force and Bishop's volume deals with a local society in Papua New Guinea. This is David Counts's discussion of monetization among the Kaliai of New Britain. Here, another factor shows itself. In pre-contact trade the Kaliai, like the Tolai, had developed a kind of shell-bead currency which functioned as general purpose money. This is also used, however, as a political tool by big men, to obtain wives for young men who then stay with them and help produce pigs and foodstuffs, which they employ in lavish mortuary feasts. Thus, 'among the Kaliai the pig is the symbol of the external aspect of big-manship' (p. 52). The people are not very dependent on trade as such for their subsistence, as they have plenty of land and also access to sea resources. The same abundance of land, however, has brought to them a massive oil-palm development where settlers from other parts of the country have come to live; and with this has come a new urban complex at the town of Kimbe. In the past people sent their copra further away, to Rabaul; now, the roads lead to and from Kimbe and copra is marketed there instead. Kaliai also sell betel-nut and lime to the settlers in the town market. In addition, despite the fact that pigs were tied up in a nexus of credit and debt in local exchanges, they were some-times willing to market cooked pork or live animals: 'one pig was sold live for K50 and the other butchered and sold in the market for K80' (p. 56). Counts goes on to make the familiar and correct point that the Kaliai are neither fundamentally conservative nor fundamentally innovative, but both. They will take new opportunities, but also wish to retain practices which give them a feeling of worth or intrinsic value. 'They attempt to contain change, not to negate it. They will ride the tiger, but they hope it can be tamed before the end of the ride' (p. 57). His conclusion indicates that it is doubtful if they will: 'The Kaliai . . . are well on their way to becoming a peasantry, with a continuous orientation to the new town and with more and more of their relations with each other (as well as with outsiders) being mediated by the need for money' (p. 58) (see also Lingenfelter, 1978).[2]

Counts's paper is a little tantalizing, because we do not learn from it whether the *vula* has disappeared or not, and if it has, why. A similar currency among the Tolai had maintained its position because it is important in funeral feasts and must be accumulated for redistribution at them. Kaliai dependence on pigs and willingness to market these could short-circuit any such mechanism and make *vula* unnecessary. But if the Kaliai, like Hageners and Pangia people, are becoming more oriented to the townships and the sale of products, it also appears that their mortuary feasts are being maintained. Again, therefore, rather than seeing traditional practices as necessarily disappearing with monetization, we have to recognize that a new interdependence may emerge between them. It is this which now requires detailed comparative study. In all the cases I have referred to, a system of chiefship or big-manship is in evidence. The development of new political and new business roles, eagerly sought after, does not appear to destroy the big-man pattern. Indeed businessmen are called big-men and are expected to behave accordingly, although they are also enabled to accumulate wealth invisibly, out of their own social system, by modern forms of investment. Here, then, is a fundamental problem: whenever a form of political legitimacy is sought, wealth has to be given away. In this sense we are merely registering the continuity of a cultural principle, which has as its basis the idea of reciprocity. Yet, as is well known, this same idea can operate to mask inequality rather than contain it. It is a hard matter, then, to decide in which cases the former rather than the latter process is now predominently occurring. From another perspective, the important matter to clarify, as I have already noted, is that of conditions of reproduction. In a process of change it may not be possible simply to pinpoint a mechanism for 'reproduction', since modification is also constantly occurring. But in general it is possible to study the extent to which the goods incorporated into exchanges themselves determine whether local autonomy is preserved or lost and in what senses. The wholesale adoption of money in the *moka* and its parallel use along with shells in Pangia, both indicate that these systems are 'dependent' on the people's cash income. At the same time their historical choice to employ goods in this way has been their own. What has changed is the direction of the lines of power, or at least their extension, as Ongka notes in the quotation at the front of this book, out to the commercial and political capital of Papua New Guinea, and beyond.

At the beginning of this study, I stated that my aim was not to approach any general theory of social change. My concern has rather been with the insights we may draw from two case studies within a single region, studied fairly continuously in the field since the 1960s. But, whatever one's immediate concerns, there is no avoiding the wider issues which underlie my descriptions, and the ghost in the machine of my account has obviously been that of Marxist theory: truly ghost-like and pale, because its teeth have almost all been drawn. I have not proceeded along the lines that 'this causes that', because I do not believe that social causes can profitably be reduced to a linear form of this kind: matters are simply too complicated.

Such a viewpoint will scarcely recommend my argument to stricter and more committed Marxists. But I have thought it worthwhile to register a position which is neither eclectic nor yet properly Marxist in any strong sense. That is, I am interested in using the concepts and insights obtained through *explicitly* Marxist studies in order to provide *implicit* baselines against which my own accounts can be measured, and I think this position marks an historical point in the acceptance of Marxist ideas within social anthropology.

Marxist models of society, social process, social change, and structure have themselves undergone a rapid phase of micro-evolution since their emergence in the last decade into the centre of social anthropological theorizing. There are defences of classical Marxism, structuralist re-interpretations of it, attempts to use the mode of production concept as a tool for the analysis of change by talking of the articulation of modes of production, and, finally there has been a resurgence of interest in the concept of social reproduction, whether or not linked to specific notions of modes of production. I doubt if these various formulations have attained greater theoretical or heuristic value than many of their predecessors. What has been bequeathed to us, however, is a much sharper concern with conflict, inequality, change, the influence of capitalism, unequal exchange, accumulation, and the like, reflecting unequivocally the end of 'modernization' as a viable theory of social change and economic development. Granted this, the traditional problems of anthropology have not been greatly altered. It is largely a matter of taste and empirical circumstance whether we choose to stress conflict or cohesion, change or persistence; the real questions of determination, and the influence between factors remain with us. An earlier anthropology spoke in terms of propositions such as 'religion reflects social structure', a kind of Africanist reformulation of Durkheim's proposition concerning Australian Aboriginal religions. Marxists of the classical persuasion carry this one step further and argue that social

structure is a precipitate of determining factors which depend ulti-
mately on the economy. But both these arguments suffer from the
arbitrary slicing up and ethnocentric reification of the data themselves.
Who is to say what is religion and what is social structure? Who is to say
what is 'the economy' as opposed to 'the religion'? It is true that we
may pin our faith on such etic concepts as we have – although they are
in truth derived from our own cultural background – attempting to
gain insight by a comparative method, but we should always remember
the slender conceptual bases on which such exercises rest. In practice,
what our efforts come down to is this: can we argue for necessary and
sufficient conditions which will explain the persistence or disappearance of any complex of customary activities? Starting with the facts of
persistence or change, can we reconstruct, through history or hypothesis, what those conditions are? The value of the 'social production'
approach is that it directs our attention precisely to such questions, and
also alerts us to the fact (or likelihood) that at all times social complexes
of activity have depended somewhat on other complexes outside themselves, for their continued existence. The Highlands social systems were
of this kind: they depended extensively on trade. Yet equally, their
forms are not susceptible to explanation simply in terms of such dependence. They themselves generated demands and placed constraints on
neighbouring systems. And their cultural specificity is not, as I have
repeatedly argued, in a one-to-one relationship with the development
of their forces and relations of production; or if it is, this relationship
remains to be stated.

But that there *is* an interplay is not in doubt, and the best way to
explore it seems to me to be in the spirit, if not the letter, of Modjeska's
examination of 'the evolving lineage mode of production' (Modjeska
1982). Where I part company with his analysis is in terms of his concentration on the lineage itself, which leads him to use the typological
notion of 'mode of production' in association with this. Without speaking of modes or even lineages, it is possible for us simply to use the idea
of 'relations of production and reproduction' which transcend the small
social units within which certain productive interests are pursued. The
wider factors of trading patterns can thus be brought back into focus,
while at the same time one looks at questions of the sexual division of
labour, hierarchy, and exploitation. On the way, aspects of culture will
no doubt be illuminated, but it remains to be seen whether a single
theory will give us the key to all cultural variation in this region. What is
needed for progress is a comprehensive understanding of the forces

underlying *both* production and exchange in these societies, and in this regard I argue that we must look for the correlates of the 'intensification' of production, not just in changing lineage structures but in wider kin relations, in terms of gender, in kinds of political leadership, and, most crucially, in responses to introduced changes. This short study has given some glimpses of how such an end might be achieved, but the topic now requires a broader form of attack which only a team of investigators could mount.

Notes

1 For comparison with the introduction of the steel axe, at an earlier stage of contact, it is interesting to consider the effects of vehicles. These certainly represent a 'technological change' and make a potential difference to production, although they are not in themselves instruments of labour (even if tractors and bulldozers are). The main point is that, essentially, cars have been treated as an important kind of valuable. This is in itself no different from the dual way in which they are categorized in western society, especially in regard to vehicles used by people of high status such as politicians, company directors, or heads of government departments. The growth of numbers of vehicles on the roads since the 1960s in the Highlands is quite remarkable, and it is not entirely, of course, to be explained by the fact that owning a car confers prestige. Vehicles are used as an essential technical part of the process by which people are linked to the external world. People travel in them predominantly to and from town, and while there they sell market produce, buy food and clothes in shops, visit banks, use telephones, and post letters, as well as meeting friends and lobbying in government offices. Without vehicles this whole process would be enormously slower, but they no more determine their use than the steel axe determined what happened in Highlands societies. Like ecology, technology is enabling or constraining: it places limits and releases possibilities, and these are realized only within a certain ideological and social context.

To make this point even stronger, we may look at the way in which the handling of vehicles has been given meaning in Hagen. First, they have been given away in *moka* and in bride-wealth. This itself suggests that they have been incorporated notionally into the framework of goods which symbolically reproduce life. Second, they are recognized as dangerous, wild things (*mel römi*). They have no mind of their own but like a wild spirit are capable of killing anyone who gets in their way. Third, however, in contradiction, they are also seen as potentially under the influence of ancestral ghosts. They must be blessed by a sacrifice when they are first put into service and if their owner becomes filled with *popokl* (anger) they may break down and prove difficult to start. All these features are products of Hagen ideas about objects of significance which are closely linked to people in a social network. None of them could be predicted without a knowledge of pre-existing cultural ideas and none is necessary as part of a functional 'adaptation' to the increased possibilities of travel afforded by vehicles. On the other hand, vehicles are used also in a definite material context. They transport large numbers of people and their goods into town and back, usually in connection with the daily market. They require petrol and servicing. People compete to get on them. Bus services have sprung up to meet the growing passenger demands. Time, money and labour are consumed in ways which take away from other activities. All these matters are obviously objective and material, and apply wherever vehicles are used. What I am suggesting here is that the particular conjunction of these universal and predictable factors with a certain set of ideas does not correspond to any systematic determination. The ideas are not a product of the use of vehicles, nor is the use pattern simply a precipitate of these. Rather, each corresponds to a different sector of determining influences which meet in peoples' actions, and are therefore pragmatically linked; they do not yield to a monocausal explanation.

2 Lingenfelter considers the colonial experience to have been the determining factor in economic development. My view is that this is a little over-simplified if it is intended as a full 'explanation' of change rather than an 'observation about' it.

Appendices

These two appendices are included partly as historical records, indicating points of analysis I developed in unpublished papers written in 1977–78, and partly because they considerably supplement the data in the main chapters themselves.

An updating comment on Appendix 1 is given in note 5 to Chapter 4. With regard to provincial government, this has developed considerably since 1978, and as my fieldwork has not been concentrated at this level I am not in a position to analyse the process in detail. Two points, however, are worth making. The Provincial Policy Secretariat has implicitly been identified with the Pangu Party at the national level, and this produced problems for it up to and immediately following the 1982 national elections. Second, a 1982 vote of 'no confidence' in the Premier was organized partly on the basis of the rift between the two language areas of the province, and partly again on a National Party versus Pangu Party basis. There is, then, 'interference' between national and provincial politics, although the Premier, Mr Nambuga-Mara tried hard to avoid this, in particular by refusing to be in his office for some weeks prior to the national elections when the National Party was fostering attempts at 'no confidence' motions in the Provincial Government because of its supposed pre-Pangu stance. Violence erupted immediately after the elections because of the success of two Ndika candidates, Mr Paias Wingti in Hagen Open and Mr Kindi Lawi in Western Highlands Provincial electorate, both Pangu members. The Provincial headquarters, occupied by the Premier and his staff, was threatened, a Pangu supporter had his house ransacked, and villagers set up road-blocks. It was rumoured that all this was the work of Mokei tribesmen, upset at the ousting of their own favoured candidates of the United Party, Mr Raphael Ndoa, the sitting Provincial MP, and Mr Michael Kundil. The provincial Premier and his ministers nevertheless proceeded to Port Moresby to see the election of the new Prime Minister, Mr Michael Somare, leader of the Pangu Party, and Mr Wingti was named by Mr Somare as his Deputy Prime Minister and Minister for Transport (subsequently National Planning and Development). Mr Wingti's cross-cousin, Mr J. Pun, was the Provincial Secretary, until the reorganization of administration which took place during 1983. In this year he became First Assistant Secretary, Policy and Planning, in the Department of Western Highlands.

Appendix 1
Village Courts in the
Dei Council area 1977

Village Courts were established in Dei by a proclamation of 21 June, 1976, and began to operate in the last week of September of that year. The division of the Council into areas followed certain patterns of administrative and political separation which had grown up since 1961.

Area 1: Muglamp

Muglamp has been the site of the government administrative centre, a police post, and a community school for several years. From 1974 onwards government officers have lived there rather than at the site of the Local Government Council itself, at Mala. Court cases have tended accordingly to be heard at Muglamp rather than Mala (or Penga, as it may more accurately be termed). This concentration of administrative activity on Muglamp has tended to reverse the previous pattern, up to 1973, when the 'Penga side' of the Council tended to receive more active supervision and interest from government workers. The shift corresponds with the translation of Mr Parua-Kuri to national political office from his position of pre-eminence in the Council, for he is from the Penga part of the area, and although he has retained office as a councillor he has not taken such a close interest in local affairs since he became an MP.

Muglamp was therefore an obvious choice for the site of a Village Courthouse. The area predominantly serves clans of two large tribes, Minembi and Kombukla, but also smaller groups from Kawelka, Kimka, Kiklpukla, and Römndi. Most of these are allied closely with the Minembi people. The Kawelka, however, from Kuk, are not really a part of the Muglamp complex, and have in fact shared their Village Court with Ndika groups in the Hagen Council area. The Kawelka are divided between Kuk, included in Muglamp court area, and Mbukl, which belongs to the Tiki court area on the 'Penga side'. Kawelka and Minembi clans are, at the inter-tribal level, traditional enemies, whereas the main Muglamp groups from Minembi and Kombukla are allies.

Area 2: Kenjipi

This comprises the north-east part of the Council, bordering with Banz at its eastern end. The tribes here tend to be clustered in alliance around the main clans of the Kendipi tribe itself, so the area has a definite unity. Candidates from Kendipi have stood in national elections since 1968. Since Parua's assumption of national political office, the Council President has also come from Kendipi tribe; he is Nori-Kumi, a previous traditional big-man. Nori died in 1982 and was greatly mourned by his fellow councillors and clansmen. Much quieter and less forceful than Parua, he did not use his presidency to maintain a Penga 'hegemony' over Dei Council as a whole.

This court area includes the resettlement block known as Konda-pina, and one of its magistrates, Kibungi-Tomben, is an Enga farmer from it. Of the other five magistrates one, Ring-Pung, is also Council Vice-President and a leader in *moka*; another, Warike-Weima, has held the position of interpreter for the Council since its inception in 1963, and also stood three times in national elections.

Area 3: Kotna

Kotna is the name of a Lutheran mission station set up in the early 1950s two miles from Penga. Thus, for many years the place has been a focus of activity. A small market, subsidiary to the main Council market at Penga, has sprung up to serve people in the hospital or health centre run by the mission. Early converts built a large church at Kotna, and the congregation now runs all its own affairs without a resident missionary. The court area serves three different sets of people: Tipuka and Welyi tribesmen, and people from Maplke, Palke, and sections of both Tipuka and Welyi in the Jimi Valley north of Kotna. (A side road into the Jimi leads past the hospital and into Welyi territory.) The Tipuka and Welyi peoples have a history of mixed relations. Tipuka men drove Welyi Katemb clan into the Jimi in warfare not long before the whole area was pacified in the 1940s, and these Welyi returned to their previous lands under the aegis of the mission, so have tended to be staunch Lutherans. Their concern with the standing of the mission station is reflected in court cases where young men have been charged with being drunk or playing cards inside the mission area. The courthouse itself stands on mission ground just behind a congregation-owned trade-store.

Area 4: Tigi

This is the most remotely situated of the court areas, and serves a mixed set of clans from Kawelka, Minembi, Kope, and Klamakae tribes. There are some uneasy traditional enmities between Kawelka and Minembi as well as certain cross-cutting alliances. Moreover, the situation chosen for the courthouse has no previous history of use for administrative work although it is quite close to the large coffee plantation at Tigi begun in 1956 by an Australian entrepreneur, and now owned by the Dei Local Government Council. Most of its workers are from other Highlands districts and provinces, and they do not have any separate representation in the magistracy of the Tigi court area. The coffee from the plantation is carried out to the town on Baiyer road rather than the Tigi road, which passes through the centre of Kawelka settlements. At the time of my visit (9–25 September 1977) the Tigi road was in very poor order, although repairs and re-cutting had apparently begun by the time I left. Factors of this kind clearly hampered the effective operation of the Village Court. In addition, within the Kawelka tribe, because of its split residence between Kuk and Mbukl, at present the major councillorship is held by a leader from the Kuk area, and a subsidiary councillorship also went to a man who spends much of his time at Kuk and is less than active in community affairs. Although the Kawelka do have a magistrate on the Tigi court panel,

Konts-Klönt, an established leader and ex-councillor, there was a general feeling that they did not truly belong to or respect it; nor could they switch to the Kotna court, which served their chief allies, the Tipuka. Certain personal shortcomings of the magistrates in Tigi may also have contributed to this lack of confidence in the court.

In summary, the court areas are as set out in *Table 1*:

Table 1 *Village court areas in Dei Council*

area	population	no. of magistrates	Peace Officers	no. of clerks
Muglamp (Gumanch)	6,460	6	2	1
Kenjipi	5,800	6	2	1
Kotna	5,340	6	2	1
Tigi	5,030	5	2	1
totals	22,630	23	8	4

Source: File no. 7-4-2, Department of Justice, Mt Hagen.

When Village Courts first began in Dei there had already been much speculation and divergent opinion among the people about the likelihood of their success. Doubts mostly centred on the question of the magistrates' ability to establish themselves both as impartial judges in the way that alien magistrates were perceived, and as men of wisdom able to guide their fellow clansmen and others as community members at the same time. In other words, potential role-shortcomings and role-conflicts were anticipated. Yet there was much interest in and support for the principle of such courts. One of the strongest arguments put up for them was that criminals would find it much harder to trick their own village magistrates, and so there would be more effective punishments. This idea was still much used by magistrates in September 1977 when I was there, and was generally accepted by then. In one of the court cases to which I listened at Kotna it was explicitly put forward by Yei, one of the magistrates who is also a traditional big-man.

Another feature of court activity which was very noticeable in the first week of operations of the court at Tigi was the tendency for magistrates to impose very heavy fines as a solution to almost all cases, without much regard to more established local ideas of compensation or shaking hands to heal a quarrel. Thus, in one case, a woman had insulted her brother's wife, and the accounts of the two women made it clear that both in fact had used rude expressions about one another. A matter of this kind would usually have been settled at home, being 'heard' by an influential family member; such a big-man would be certain to point out that both women had done wrong and argue that they should make a direct exchange of money to 'shake hands'; he would also have told them not to quarrel again. The magistrates in the case I watched, however, did none of these things. They simply ordered the clerk to look up the penalty in his book, and when he said 'K50' they imposed this as a fine on the defendant, and immediately added that she would have to go to gaol if she could not find the amount at once. She had K30 ready, as it happened, and was forced to appeal to her husband's kin to get the rest. The impression of harshness which I formed then was reinforced in all subsequent cases during the day, and at its end, the magistrates spoke proudly of how much money would be going into the Local Government Council bank. Later, one of them added that some of it could later be used to increase the wages of magistrates and/or to help develop their area. The possibility that magistrates might think in this way does not seem to have been ancitipated in the debates prior to the setting up of Village Court legislation. The second alternative, however, that fine money can be used to help the areas from which the fines are drawn, is no doubt realized in the Kainantu Village Courts of the Eastern Highlands, where they are linked to Komuniti Kaunsil areas.

I asked friends at home in the clan area about the pattern of hearing cases and imposing fines of that day. Nikint, a man I have known for thirteen years, who is now in his early thirties, said forcefully that: first, the manner of appointment of the Tigi magistrates and others had been wrong and that some responsibility for this was to be borne by the Mt Hagen Administration, who had set the matter up without proper consultation of the Kawelka people at Mbukl and Golke; second, some of the magistrates were not truly important or significant men and their appointment was wrong; and third, if courts were held like this all the time, people would stop taking cases to those magistrates, so the purpose of the court would be defeated, for people would still go instead to the Local Court magistrates at Muglamp or in Mt Hagen town.

Nikint was not opposed in principle to the courts. Indeed, he had been so keen on them as to hope that perhaps if a proper election for magistrates were held, he could stand in order to become one. One could argue that his views were based on disappointment; but they coincided with my own perception of the situation. It should be noted, though, that my concern was the result of observations at only one courthouse, Tigi. Subsequent work in 1977 suggests that the work of these courts has been highly variable, and that there is indeed a strong need to ensure regular methods of supervision of court work by responsible Local Court magistrates. This point has already been recognized in the Department of Justice at Mount Hagen, by Mr Phillip Eka and Mr Bob Welsh. It was with little surprise that I learned from the official file on the Dei courts that the people had requested replacement of one of the Tigi magistrates, as they were dissatisfied with his work. This particular man, from Yelipimbo clan officially based at Mbukl, was drunk during the first sitting of the court in September 1976. The example is by no means an isolated one.

During a return visit to Dei I attempted directly to follow up my initial observations. The Kawelka people in Tigi court area were fairly quiet about the court's progress. They were glad to have their own man, Kont, still as magistrate, but pointed out that court sessions were not being held regularly, and that not many people were using the court. On two occasions when I visited the courthouse in expectation of observing cases, these views were confirmed. No courts were held; people were drinking nearby; and the key to the trade-stores in which court order books were kept had been taken to town by the trade-store owner. The courthouse itself had no door so that nothing could be kept inside it. A friend, however, suggested that the Kotna court was better run, because 'only some of the magistrates are drinkers' and because it was near a place where 'law is respected' so that the magistrates could not 'humbug too much'. This was clearly true. The Kotna courthouse was built of sawn timber and had a galvanized iron roof and a lockable door, with walls of plaited cane and a cement floor. The clerk's desk was high, rather like a judge's bench, and there was an air of sobriety and relative efficiency about the place. Nevertheless, on one of the days it was supposed to sit, its clerk had gone off to Lae without making alternative arrangements or telling the magistrates, and the upshot was that I observed only one full court session during my two weeks in the field, at Kotna on 13 September, 1977.

As has been noted for elsewhere, people were gathered on grassy banks and under the shade of trees near the courthouse, 'trying out' cases with the help of men who held the position of *komiti* under the Council system. (It is my understanding that the people consider this system to have officially lapsed since Village Courts were introduced, but 'unofficially' it continues to play an obviously relevant role in sorting cases and presenting evidence in actual Village Court hearings, since members have experience in handling disputes). In some places this function is apparently carried by the Peace Officers. This was not so in Kotna, nor was it likely to be so. The two Peace Officers there are definitely young toughies, ready to pinion the arms of a struggling defendant reluctant to face the court and to slam the door on someone as he is pushed into the 'room-guard' just next to the actual court hearing room. One of the two had previously been dubbed 'army man' by a leader at Mbukl from whom he appears to have stolen a number of pigs by creeping through the bush in the manner of an attacking guerilla force. Both Peace Officers, then, seemed to fit the image of strong 'policemen' rather than 'peace men'. They are known, as are all such officers in Hagen, as the court's *el nde wuö* (policemen).

The two Peace Officers also reinforced the demands of the magistrates that defendants stand up straight and face the desk when talking; that they should not interject, interrupt, or directly contradict other people's evidence until called on to speak; and that they should go quietly into the lock-up room and not communicate with people outside once in it, a rule which itself conflicted patently with the urgent need of some of those convicted to raise money for fines instead of being gaoled. As a result, numerous hurried conversations were held through the open louvres of the 'room-guard's' windows by prisoners seeking assistance from relatives. If they raised their voices too loud, the Peace Officers shouted warnings to them and also checked out the front of the courthouse, threatening people talking around it with gaol for contempt of court. Bystanders joked about this, but kept a wary eye open in case one of the Peace Officers should really mean it.

'Orderly procedure' within the actual courthouse was thus, by and large, maintained. Not all the cases 'tried out' actually reached the court; and not all the matters brought to the court had been 'tried out' first. Some were only preliminary notices of matter to be heard later. On the 13th the main case heard was an accusation of pig theft. Others were: a money debt owed by a young man of Tipuka Oklembo clan to an ancient neighbour, Pöng, of T. Kitepi clan (the two clans form an ally pair); a case over the sale of black market beer inside the mission station; a case referred again to the court concerning a disturbance at a party held by one of the Village Court magistrates in the mission area;

and a dispute between a husband and wife which was referred to a later hearing because the husband was not present.

There are six magistrates for this court. Wara-Reia of Kotna, who is Chairman of the Village Court, an established minor big-man, who was already a *komiti* in 1964 and continues to be a councillor for his clan, Wendandarakl, in the Welyi tribe. Ongka-Opa of Ambukla, is a traditional big-man of the Tipuka Kelmbo clan, and an attractive orator who has succeeded in overcoming the handicap of a partly-withered right arm. He does not seem to be active in the Village Court, though, which is a pity, as he is usually a full participant in any important inter-clan discussions, including disputes, which are held outside the official court context. It is possible his manner is too flamboyant to suit the atmosphere of a small, cement-floored courthouse. Rumba-Kumbukl of Kera in the Jimi Valley, is from a section of the Welyi tribe who are in the Jimi. He is quiet, and although a councillor, is not a big-man. Kumi-Ko of Rulna is a magistrate not known to me personally. He is also from the Jimi, but does not seem to turn up often for court work. Engk-Ok of Nunga No 2, is a long-standing *komiti* from one section of the Kitepi clan to which the MP also belongs. His father was an outstanding polygamist big-man. Engk is sturdy and outspoken, and has many years of experience in dispute settlement. Yei-Jimi of Kints, belongs to Kengeke clan in Tipuka tribe, and is an important big-man of one sub-clan in it. He is an excellent speaker, eloquent, humorous, and patient and is obviously very sound as a magistrate. He and Engk appear to provide the essential 'backbone' for the court. Both have enough weight to give well-accepted advice and reproval to defendants in court cases.

The influence of the last two magistrates named, Engk and Yei, was shown clearly in the pig theft dispute which was the main case heard on the 13th. Engk was at first inclined to assist the defendant, who comes from his own mother's group, the Minembi Yelipimbo. He cross-examined the chief witness against the defendant and argued that she should have reported the theft and her evidence of it earlier. She is married to the defendant's elder brother, but herself comes from a group with some scores to pay off against the defendant, since they think he has stolen their pigs before. However, the weight of evidence from the owner of the lost pig, a *komiti* of his group, plus reported testimony from three other men of the defendant's own group, all pointed rather clearly to his guilt. While Engk was still stalling on some minor points Yei cut in on the discussion to say quite firmly that the reputation of the defendant was very clear. Yei's own clan 'looked after' the defendant's clan by providing it with land when its men were driven away in warfare, and as neighbours they knew all about one another's affairs, so he had heard long ago about the defendant's thefts and adulteries. In this instance he had seduced his own wife's brother's wife and when pressed for a pig in compensation had stolen a pig from his sister's husband's people in Minembi Mimke clan and given it to them. The scandal of this was passed quickly to all nearby groups. In court, however, the defendant denied everything, right to the end. Engk pointed out to him that his *own* people were witnesses against him, so what could the magistrates say? Yei said he thought the defendant should have four months in gaol, not ten weeks, to teach him a lesson, and he was shunted into the 'room-guard', reappearing thereafter several times with vain appeals to be allowed to pay a partial fine instead of going to jail. At the end of the court session at 10 o'clock the only remaining problem was how actually to transport their prisoner to Muglamp to hand him over to police. It did not seem to occur to the magistrates as a possibility that they could ask for help from the nearby police station at Yan (about two and a half miles from Kotna Village Court on the main north Wahgi road) where transport is sometimes available.

The actual case involved here, pig theft, is not among the most commonly handled categories of cases in the Kotna court. I was permitted by its officials to study the court order books, and from these a breakdown on types of cases heard has been prepared (*Table 2*). Closer analysis of the categories is needed, but it is immediately clear that cases of debt predominate over matters of theft, and that disputes centering on relations between the sexes are also prominent.

Some of the cases are inadequately represented in the categories I have adopted; thus my category 'husband-wife disputes' contains a variety of actual situations, including separation or desertion, insults, and assaults, which, unless there is a separate charge of assault, I do not record also as assault. The category of assault itself combines insults and threats with actual physical attacks. 'Drunk and disorderly' also covers many cases of insult and assault. Unlawful intercourse mostly relates to adultery but there are one or two cases where the marital status of the people involved is not clear. This category also includes some instances which would be classifiable as rape or close to rape, where the woman is said not to have agreed to the act. In one case a wife complained that her husband forced her and tore off her apron, and he was instructed to

Table 2 *Categories of cases heard at Kotna Village Court 23 September, 1977, recorded on form 6 and settlement orders*

category		form 6 orders	settlement orders	totals
A	debts	22	26	48
B	damages, assault, and insult	19	10	29
C	theft	9	6	15
D	miscellaneous:			
	resis tok	11	6	5
	playing cards	8	2	10
	drunk and disorderly	14	—	14
	breaking Council rules	3	—	3
	wage disputes	—	1	1
E	male-female relations:			
	divorce	1	3	4
	husband-wife disputes	4	9	13
	unlawful intercourse	11	2	13
	other	—	—	—
F	contempt of court	7	—	7
totals		79	66	145

pay her compensation as well as paying a fine to the court. In cases of this kind supervising magistrates could perhaps suggest that the matter should be referred as a criminal charge to a higher court, if the circumstances appear serious enough to warrant this. It is a fact, however, that the handling of such cases in the Village Court closely parallels customary ideas in the Mt Hagen area; to wit, that in unlawful intercourse it is the fact of such intercourse that is significant and requires compensation, rather than the degree of force used to obtain it. A women's consent is relevant: if intercourse is with her consent, she will be punished too. But if she does not give consent, it is presumed that the man uses force and not much attention is paid to his degree of culpability by questioning 'how much force'.

The cases involving breaking Council rules, playing cards, drunkenness, and contempt of court were almost invariably brought before the court by a magistrate or officer of the Kotna court itself; in one instance a case was brought against the Peace Officer of another court in the Dei area. Otherwise, however, court officers were not prominent in prosecuting, and when magistrates did bring cases, they did so much as private citizens would. Similarly, in one case I observed a magistrate was subject to prosecution during the day's proceedings. However, he successfully explained his position to the others – that he had not instigated a troublesome beer-party – and the matter was dropped.

The one wage dispute I witnessed was brought by a car driver against his employer from the Welyi group – a complaint of non-payment of wages. The relations between car owners and their drivers tend to be informal, and often the driver is a relative, if not of the same group. If wages are not paid the driver either 'humbugs' and bumps the car or takes it on long journeys without permission in search of female companions, or else simply gives up in a huff. So, although non-payment is actually frequent, it does not often emerge into the arena of disputes in court.

It may now be worthwhile to look in a little more detail at the more commonly occurring categories (see *Table 2*). First, debts (A). Often cases related to some time in the past: one, two, or several years. As can be seen, almost all were made the subject of settlement orders, i.e. when a case was brought the debtor almost always seems to have agreed rapidly to pay, and the plaintiff was satisfied with a promise to settle it at home by a certain date. The two debt cases handled under form 6 both involved money; of those recorded under settlements, 18 concerned pigs or primarily pigs, 7 money, and 1 a cassowary. Settlement in terms of money rather than in kind was noted as acceptable in a number of these cases. It is not possible to tell whether the litigants were also exchange partners or not; though it would be interesting, and quite significant to do so, since partners in *moka* exchange are not supposed to 'make a court out of debts' in a system supposedly imbued with ideals of honour and credit. My guess is that the bulk of these debts fell outside the formal nexus of *moka* partnerships. I also think it likely that the court in its first year dealt with a backlog of such cases which could not be handled effectively by other means. On the other hand, it is possible that the availability of redress through the courts will alter the code of *moka*-making and lead to a mass of court complaints after an unsuccessful *moka* (or even a successful one since there is *always* some dissatisfaction with gifts).

Damages, assault, and insult (B) is a rather broadly defined category. A closer breakdown of the figures is shown in *Table 3*.

The property damages almost invariably involved garden damage done by pigs. Damages to people by assault probably often refer to

Table 3   *Damages*

	form 6 orders	settlement orders	totals
damages to property	2	7	9
damages to persons, by assault, insult or other dangerous acts	17	3	20
totals	19	10	29

cases where drinking is involved, although many of these are recorded under 'drunk and disorderly'. Assaults were often accompanied, or sparked off, by insults, as might be expected. 'Other dangerous acts' refers to a case in which a man was reported to the court for making a pig trap, consisting of a pit with spiked bamboos set in its floor, into which one of the Kotna magistrates fell. The maker of the trap agreed to compensate the magistrate. If we note again that there are cases involving interpersonal violence both in categories B (assault) and D (drunk and disorderly), sometimes in E (husband-wife disputes and unlawful intercourse), and quite often also in F (contempt of court) (since the Peace Officers laid this kind of charge against those who struggled with them or hit them when arrested), it becomes clear that there is an element of such violence in at least fifty of the cases handled, or approximately a third of the total. The figure is not of course rigidly established, but it suggests that instances of violence are fairly common, a conclusion in line with our knowledge of patterns of self-assertion and aggressiveness in the society as a whole. The sub-category *resis tok* or *tok kros* in D could also be included under 'insult', to add further weight to this impression.

In category E, male-female relations, the cases of actual divorce are much less frequent than complaints between husband and wives not leading to divorce, or at least not leading to it in the time space of these cases. Such cases of divorce as were handled by the court seem to have been very much *faits accomplis* by the time the cases were heard, and three of the four were accordingly handled simply as settlement orders, agreed between the spouses. The husband-wife disputes ranged from quarrels with elements of rape, assault, and insult, to desertion of spouses, or neglect and failure to support the spouse and children.

In most instances a quarrel with some insult element was reported. One of the 'other' cases here, was a 'breach of promise to marry' case, which is interesting, since such cases are not common. The important point about this one was that the prospective wife had been helped by the man's parents to buy a ticket to go to Port Moresby to be with him, and they were really most interested in recovering what had become a debt, since once there, she had not stayed with their son for long.

The one divorce case in E which was dealt with on form 6 had to do with a man who 'greased' his daughter to leave her husband and marry another man. So the charge was really against him for breaking up a marriage. The 'unlawful intercourse' category includes examples of attempts at this as well as cases of success. An 'attempt' may be harder to prove, but in Hagen customary law such a case may lead to a request for compensation, although not as much as when the act is completed.

In addition to this summary of the kinds of cases decided it may be useful to include some information on the pattern of sentencing the magistrates followed (*Table 4*). The categories are the same as those in *Table 2*. More cases have been assigned to the assault/threat/damage category, however (22 against 18); into unlawful intercourse (12 as against 11); and into husband-wife disputes (5 as against 4). This is sometimes because what were counted as single cases in *Table 2* carried more than one set of sentences, so these are counted separately for *Table 4*. On the other hand, fewer cases of drunken behaviour and of contempt of court appear. Some have been re-assigned to the assault category. Different ways of counting the units of new data probably explain such minor discrepancies as remain in my notes and are re-flected in a lack of exact correspondence between *Tables 2* and *4*.

The average sizes of fines imposed through the various categories are: A —; B K40; C K40; D K7 (playing cards), K7 (breaking Council rules), K50 (*resis tok* – only one case), K30 (drunk and disorderly); E K37 (unlawful intercourse), K50 (husband-wife disputes); F K40; the average of the averages is K33. The theoretical maximum fine which a Village Court can impose is K50 for one offence. Those in excess of this recorded here may implicitly relate to more than one offence; or the clerk may have failed to record a 'compensation' element to be deducted from the actual fine. If so, this would confirm my impression from listening to a court session and talking to people that there is uncertainty about fines *vis-à-vis* compensation, although the distinction is made in the clerk's Pidgin terminology of *baim ofis* (fine) and *baim man/meri* (compensation). However that may be,

Table 4 *Sentencing patterns, Kotna Village Court 1976–77 (form 6 orders)*

category	fine imposed or community work	compensation	gaoled if failed to pay or work
A debts	—	to repay debt	—
	—	K40 to repay debt	—
B damages	—	K4	—
	K40	to repay pig killed	—
assault, insult, threat	K50	—	—
	K50 or 1 month's work	K30	—
	K50	—	—
	K50	—	—
	K50	—	—
	K30	—	—
	K50	—	—
	K30	K20	—
	K50	—	—
	K50	—	—
	K50	—	—
	K50	—	—
	2 weeks' work	—	—
	K60	K40	—
	K60	K60	—
	K50	K50 (wife to husband)	—
	—	K40 (son to father)	—
	K20	—	—
	K10	—	—
	K40	—	—
	K40	—	—
C theft	K20 (13 men each to pay this amount, beer)	—	—
	K20 (beer)	—	—
	K4 (spade)	K4	—
	5 weeks' work (K3)	—	—

(continued)

Table 4—*continued*

category	fine imposed or community work	compensation	gaoled if failed to pay or work
C theft—*continued*	K50 (sweet potato)	—	—
	K50 (money)	to repay K70	—
	K10 (pandanus)	K30	—
	K20 (banana)	to repay	—
	K100 (coffee)	—	—
	K100 (pig)	—	—
	K30 (3 men, banana)	K20 each	—
D playing cards	K4 each (10 men)	—	—
	K4	—	—
	K6	—	—
	K10	—	—
	K20	—	—
	K5	—	—
	K5	—	—
	K5	—	—
(resis tok)	K50	Pig worth K50 to man wrongly accused of theft	—
(breaking council rules)	K5	—	—
	K5	—	—
	K10	—	—
(drunk and disorderly)	K10	—	—
	K50	—	—
	K50	—	—
	K20	—	—
	K50	K20 to owner of damaged car	—
	K50	—	—
	K20	—	—
	K10	—	—
	K10	—	—
E unlawful intercourse	K20 (men and women)	Pigs to husband or women (man)	—

(continued)

Table 4—*continued*

category		fine imposed or community work	compensation	gaoled if failed to pay or work
E	unlawful	K10 (man)	K60 to if	—
	intercourse—	K50 (man)	—	—
	(continued)	K50 (man)	—	—
		K50 (man)	Pig to husband	—
	(same case)	K40 (girl)	—	—
		K50 (man)	—	—
	(same case)	K20 (woman)	K30 to husband (woman)	—
		K10 (man)	K30 to husband (man)	—
		K40 (man)	K40 to woman	—
		K50 (man)	—	—
		K50 (man)	—	—
		K50	—	—
	husband-wife	K50 (wife)	—	—
	disputes	K50 (wife)	Pig worth K50 to husband	—
		K50 (man who 'greased' wife)	Pig to husband	—
		—	K50 to husband for assault	—
		—	K40 to husband for assault	—
	divorce	—	—	—
F	contempt of court	K50	—	—
		K20 (13 men each)	—	—
		K50	—	—
		K40	—	—
		K20	—	—
		K60	—	—

there are 5 fines recorded in excess of the maximum (3 of K60 and 2 of K100). In the latter 2 cases I strongly suspect that part of the K100 is compensation. Aside from these instances, there are 29 cases of K50 fines, 6 of K40, 3 of K30, 11 of K20, 9 of K10, 1 of K6, 5 of K5 and 3 of K4. The predominance of maximum fines over the whole range of categories of offences is clear. In 6 cases compensation alone was ordered; in 21 a fine and compensation. As might be expected from customary procedures, the punishment of fine and compensation was particularly frequent in category C (theft) – 5 out of 11 cases, and in category E (sexual relations) – 8 out of 11. It is rather less frequent in category B (assault) – 6 out of 20. A much closer analysis of all of these cases would be needed to elucidate the internal reasons for the magistrate's decision to include a compensation order or not, and to see whether they were guided by indigenous customary concepts and attitudes or by other considerations. This, of course, is the kind of information which cannot be drawn from bare court records, but only by detailed observation and discussion of cases. I would suggest that where magistrates ordered a fine without compensation they may have seen themselves as operating in terms of the introduced model of justice prevalent from the times of the kiaps' patrols onwards, and that the fine is seen as like a gaol sentence (indeed non-payment of it in these cases led to jailing in 7 instances). The kinds of fines imposed in the unlawful intercourse category are also interesting, in that a system of fining makes it easier to punish women involved if they are guilty of 'greasing' men i.e. inciting them to have intercourse. Thus, in one case a girl was fined K40 while the man was fined K50, neither paid, and both were gaoled; and in another a married woman was required to pay K30 compensation to her husband and a K20 fine. She was gaoled, rather predictably, as she may have found it hard to raise the money from a source other than her husband. The man involved paid a smaller fine, as it was recognized, I would say from the court record, that the women had 'greased' him, but he was still separately liable to pay K30 to the husband. This again is in accordance with customary law procedures in such cases. In others where there was a large fine (K50) and no compensation, the girls will have been unmarried, I think, although again the court records as such do not enable one to say this definitely. In such cases, too, it is always the man who pays, and there is invariably an element of assault or rape present, so these could also have been classified under that category.

The overall pattern of sentencing is: fines alone, 51 cases; fine or community work, 1 case; community work alone, 2 cases; fine and compensation 21 cases; compensation alone 6 cases; no fine or compensation, 1 case. Thus the order of preference is fines; fines and compensation; compensation; community work. Fining alone is clearly very predominant indeed. The punishment of community work seems almost redundant. The difficulties of overseeing such work, even if it is to be done at the local police station or the Local Government Council buildings, are far too great for this to be an effective punishment, and magistrates no doubt know this. The general concern of court officers that the court should impress itself on the people also no doubt explains the pattern of heavy fines imposed, since this is one of the few immediately effective weapons they have to hand. Talk of putting people in gaol is also frequently used by magistrates to assert themselves, as in the pig theft case which I observed, and gaol was in fact quite a frequent outcome of the cases recorded. The gaol order book records 40 imprisonments between 23 September, 1976, and 30 August, 1977, and 20 of these derive from the present set of 82 cases recorded in *Table 5*. The gaol sentences were as given in *Table 5*.

The favourite gaol sentences are thus clearly 4 or 8 weeks. In the pig theft case observed the magistrate, Yei, suggested that the defendant

Table 5 *Gaol sentences imposed by Kotna Village Court*

sentence (weeks)	no of instances
1	2
2	2
3	1
4	18
5	4
6	1
7	0
8	14
9	0
10	0
11	0
12	4
	48

Note: Average 5.73 weeks

should have 3 or 4 months, not 10 weeks, and this kind of sentiment is quite frequently expressed by magistrates seeking to establish a 'tough' and 'impartial' image for themselves. The concern of the magistrates is no doubt related to suspicions entertained by government officers before the courts were set up that magistrates might take bribes; by policemen that they might favour their *wantoks*; and by the people at large that they might do all these things and be inefficient and unacquainted with proper procedures. Hence the efforts of 'strong' magistrates such as Yei to dispel any such views. The concern is related also to the tolerance people show to the rather high-handed actions of the Peace Officers. The overall set of concerns was shown clearly at a meeting between court officers and the Minister for Justice, Mr Delbe-Biri, in which officers asked for uniforms and handcuffs, and magistrates for more support plus transport facilities to send people to gaol in town. A police circular recognizes certain problems in this sphere, and the police at Yan station declared that they did send transport when they could, but I strongly doubt the effectiveness of the arrangements they have. An experienced old policeman from Chimbu based at Yan said to me that he did not know if the Village Court magistrates heard *prenkot* (biased courts) or what, and that he felt that the winds of crime and disorder could easily blow over the centre-post of law unless it were securely fastened on more than one side by lashings (by the ordinary police force as well as the Village Court officers). This was an issue already apparent to me by September 1976, and one which obviously continues to be important.

Conclusions and Recommendations

1   Some of the courts in Dei Council appear to be working well, largely because of a sensible choice of site for the courthouse and an equally sensible choice of magistrates. Those that are not working are likely to have been set up without a proper procedure of consultation on these two matters. From the example I know, it is possible that people consider the local MP and some of the councillors had too much of a hand in nominating magistrates, and that micro-political interests were involved. This point is worth noting, but it is not confirmed. The general point is that careful and democratic selection procedures and correct siting are essential if the Village Court is to have a chance of succeeding.

2   Magistrates and Peace Officers have not been given elaborate training, and this shows in some uncertainty about procedures, e.g. in
relation to the size of fines, gaoling, and the division of sentences into
fine and compensation. Discussion groups should be set up, to be run
by the Department of Justice, and attended by a departmental representative of the Local Court magistracy, and the Village Court
officers. In addition, the public at large is not well enough informed.
Peace Officers should discuss the limits to which they should go in
bringing people to court.

3   Courts that are not working well do not always lack good potential
magistrates; but they tend to be badly situated, and do not receive
visits from supervising magistrates regularly enough. I suggest that
supervising magistrates should be given the facilities and encouragement, and if necessary the instruction, to visit more often and to
familiarize themselves more closely with decisions of the Village Courts
and the reasons for them. They should then also help the people to
formulate more clearly any developments in their customary law which
they see as desirable and feasible as a result of operating their own
Village Courts. They should also advise on what cases such as assault
and rape should be referred to other courts.

4   There should be regular and effective liaison between police and
the Village Courts. Police could perhaps visit and get to know how the
courts are working, without actually imposing themselves on them or
taking over their running. This might help the Peace Officers. I am not
prepared to say, on the basis of my very limited fieldwork, whether
these officers should have a uniform and handcuffs. There is perhaps a
danger of 'officializing' the Village Courts too much, and so losing
sight of their potentially valuable function as venues of mediation.

5   It appears from this area that *komiti* men are still needed to help in
dispute settlement. This position should be clarified.

6   Most of the disputes dealt with in the courts are 'minor'. It is hard
to say whether they have really helped prevent large-scale conflicts in
the area. Elsewhere, it would appear that they have not. More research
work is needed on this.

7   More work is also needed on the thinking of the magistrates on
compensation as a mode of sentencing. The court cases provide only a
'skeleton' of information which needs to be fleshed out with more

discussion of attitudes and reasons. People's degree of satisfaction with decisions also needs to be further explored, and to be related to the degree of informal discussion still taking place out of court.

8   The question of what is done with money from fines is potentially a tense one. Much more information about this needs to be communicated to the people, and this could be done on court days by Local Government Council officials. There are genuine and as yet unbroached policy issues involved here. Further, there should be an examination of whether community work could be made feasible. The general consideration underlying this point is whether in some way court fines can be 'ploughed back' to help the local area itself and even, if possible, to find projects that might reduce the incidence of cases the courts have to deal with. In other words, at present (1978) the courts in this area do not have quite the integrated community functions they potentially could have.

Appendix 2
Provincial Government in the Western Highlands as seen from Dei Council in 1978

Dei Council is one of three in the Mt Hagen area of Western Highlands Province, the other two being Hagen and Mul. Established in 1962, it was originally designed to be paired, and subsequently amalgamated with Mul as a part of an envisaged general process of political consolidation. The opposite, however, occurred: following disputes over a killing and subsequent attempts at revenge, and despite elaborate and strenuous efforts at settlement via compensation payments, Dei and Mul became hostile, and since then have pursued their separate ways (A. J. Strathern 1974: 250–59; 1976b: 269–71). There are closer links with Hagen Council, realized through patterns of ceremonial exchange, resettlement, and commerce; but Dei Council people have, since its beginning, always felt themselves separate, poised between the 'metropolis' of Hagen and the plantation lands of the Wahgi, a feeling which influences their attitudes to each new issue, including that of the Provincial Government.

The Council now contains some 24,000 people, and since 1972 has also formed a separate Open electorate, returning its own MP, Mr Parua-Kuri, to the National Parliament. The Council is strung out on ridges and flats between the Waghi and the Baiyer Valleys and, in a northward sweep, includes also all the Melpa-speaking people of the Jimi Valley beyond the Sepik Wahgi Divide. To the south, its border lies along the Glumant (Gumanch) River, which flows out from Mul Council into the Wahgi; along the river bank are clustered resettlement sites of groups and fragments of groups from both north and south, and it is through this interchange area that the major links with Hagen Council people are made. Obviously, in an area whose borders touch on at least three different languages (Enga, Maring, Wahgi), it is unwise to generalize about what 'the people think'. My own work has been done from Mbukl and Golke, both belonging to the Kawelka tribe, and lying in the northern half of the Council. The Kawelka have, however, resettled in their ancestral territory of Kuk, south of the Glumant, so my identification with them has enabled, and in fact obliged me, to travel frequently to the southern half. In this way I have gained some perspective on people's views, but my information is nevertheless strongly influenced by the alliances and preferences of the Kawelka. I shall therefore explain these, and build them explicitly into the analysis itself.

The main points I wish to bring out in the account are:

(1) The models of political and economic development which have resulted from colonial and post-colonial policies have coincided in terms of an 'image of limited good', with corresponding pictures of dependency and relative advantage.
(2) These models have been largely experienced through, and also further complicated by, the operation of the Local Government Council and the location of administrative facilities.
(3) The role of the Dei MP has therefore always been a potentially ambivalent one; uncertainty about this role is likely to be increased by provincial government arrangements. Correspondingly, a similar ambivalence will surround the provincial members themselves.
(4) The correlate of this situation in people's attitudes is to be found in two contradictory circumstances: at an individual level, doubt about the likely effectiveness of provincial government, and on the corporate one, an emergent wish to split the province and form two different Provincial Governments.

Despite the apparent pessimism of these, it should be added that the process of setting up government at provincial level was being carried out cautiously and without too much fanfare during the latter half of 1978. It is possible, then, that major organizational problems will be ironed out by the time the first full-scale elections are held (either in 1979 or 1980). Structural difficulties of the kind I discuss here, however, will have to be faced, otherwise the new form of government will not effectively do anything more for the people than the established structures, despite the obvious cost.

Government and development

Ian Hughes has recently argued that the actions of Europeans in bringing large quantities of shell wealth into the Highlands from the 1930s to the 1980s set the pattern of overall dependency which is still strongly entrenched in people's attitudes: 'As the economic, social, and political consequences of the new wealth diffused outwards with the wealth-objects themselves, it was the Europeans who were always the conspicuous point of origin, the obvious initiators of change' (Hughes 1978: 318).

Hughes's argument has to be carefully sifted. There is a major measure of truth in it, from the most general viewpoint of hindsight. The 'facts' on which he reports with excellent detail I set out much earlier (A. J. Strathern 1971b: xii, 102 – 11; 1976a: 278 ff.), without the same stress on 'dependency-producing effects' in local populations. To balance Hughes's interpretation, one needs to note that internally, in Hagen society at least, the influx loosened the grip of established big-men. It also enabled groups as a whole to enter into and compete with the *moka* exchange system. There was thus a certain gain, as well as a loss, of autonomy. Hageners do not see Europeans as having introduced *moka* along with pearl shells, rather they see themselves as having seized opportunities afforded by European actions to increase their prestige through an enlarged scope of action. It is precisely this, in fact, which has subsequently led them from step to step in the development process, increasing their overall dependence *pari passu* with the perceived individual success or failure of ambitious entrepreneurs. We need to distinguish, in fact, points of origin from 'initiators of change'. Europeans were certainly seen as the former, but did not hold a monopoly of the latter.

Hughes's statement, then, must be taken at a macro-level: *overall*, Europeans were seen as the sources of increased wealth. They were, as Hageners said, 'the valuables people' (*mel-wamb*). As initial exploration turned into a more settled form of administration, and forays in search of gold were replaced by purchases of land for plantations and mission centres, the new influx took on a stable geographical pattern, disruptive of earlier ones (A. J. Strathern 1971c; Hughes 1978: 312). New centres and peripheries were created. Each European settler or missionary became, in small, what 'the government' was in large: a source of valued goods.

The significance of Europeans as possessors of valuables must, as both Hughes and I have insisted, be properly appreciated. Instead of receiving valuables only as a part of ceremonial exchange, people could produce pigs or direct labour to receive them, adjusting their demands in accordance with their productive capacities and the Europeans' perceived ability to pay. Europeans were seen as prior possessors of wealth; they were not seen as themselves having laboured to obtain it; they were the 'root-people' of valuables (*mel-nga pukl wamb*). In comparison with them, therefore, everyone became like a worker who strove through direct production to obtain valuables, sometimes literally as a wage paid at a monthly or piece-work rate. It is in this structural transformation of exchange partnership into wage-work that the origin of dependency-thinking has to be seen. There is little evidence that at first the relationship was seen in this way; it is only gradually that people grasp their true position.

The crucial factor to add is that the government was seen as the supreme version of European power, and the sources of its obvious wealth were as hidden from Hageners as was the case for missions and plantations; indeed, more so, since the govenment did not directly seek to extract economic value by running commercial business. The government could command direct inputs of labour, notably on work on the roads and house-building, but it did not, then, proceed to use such roads or houses for money-making purposes. Its capacity to pay, in spite of this, could only reinforce the appreciation of its power. Equally odd was the government's occasional refusal to pay anything for services, with the argument that all was being done 'for the people's own development'. Local Government Councils were subsequently designed to make this phase of development a reality, although not before missions and European enterprise had been given substantially more than a head start.

One can see contradictions in the concept of the Council, from its beginning. Administration policy was to introduce councils at the first stage of a process of political and, secondarily, economic education.

People would learn how to conduct democratic elections of representatives and these would find ways of debating together and managing the affairs of a wider set of local groups than were accustomed previously to any joint participation in overt decision-making. Yet 'democratic' election was bound to make more crude the subtle processes by which leaders emerged in Hagen clans, presuming, as it did, a single act of acclaim or choice and a single leader. The process of debate, while pertaining to much larger social entities than before, would then involve only a tiny handful of men, and no women. And although the whole structure was set up in order to foster 'self-reliance', in fact councillors were to spend much time debating what would be done with monies obtained via the Administration, and listening to 'experts' from government departments advising on ways in which such money should be spent. Over time, these circumstances changed: money did build up through tax and, more recently, as a result of the Council's purchase of expatriate plantations. Then the wider masses began to be more suspicious of Council doings. It is interesting, in retrospect, to note that, while councillors wished to claim parity with kiaps (government officers) – something the latter would not grant, reinforcing their reluctance by putting councillors themselves in gaol from time to time – the people have not generally accorded the Council status as a kind of 'government'. Rather, 'the councillors' are seen as one institution, and 'government' as another, located in the District Office and represented by officials.[1] Nor has the Council been seen very directly as a mini-Parliament, even though such a model has clearly been available since the national House of Assembly was created. Instead, the MP's role has taken on a very great importance as the true link with the origin-places of power.

Nevertheless, in its early years, the Council worked well enough (see A. J. Strathern 1970). The area was in need of numerous minor improvements which the Council could undertake. For instance, basic road-building was still to be done; few places had access even to a primary school; aid post networks had to be expanded. All this the Council did. Moreover, in the 1960s people were still willing to work directly on communal projects, and kiaps patrolled to see that work was kept up. A kiap was stationed at Dei Council chambers, and one particularly energetic and industrious officer (Mr R. Gleeson) saw to the construction of a new permanent building for the Council to meet in and supporting dwelling houses for its officers: clerks, translators, carpenters, and drivers. Initially tax was set at £1 10s for men and 5s for women. It subsequently rose, with the general increase in cash-cropping and the demands of the Council's programme, to $10 for males, and attempts were made at tax-payers' meetings to push it even higher. Again, this process carried with it dangers for the Council system itself. First, people became less keen on community work, which had provided an enormous 'economic subsidy' for the Council and was indeed a genuine form of self-reliance. They announced their preference to devote themselves to business and let the Council pay workers to maintain the roads. Second, either through mismanagement or a certain creeping level of malpractice, or both, the Council actually found it difficult to run its vehicles and pay workers. Kiaps were withdrawn as overseers. Executive Officers replaced them, but were without the kiaps' coercive powers. Big men continued to seek election as councillors, and some younger men emerged partly through councillorship as new big men, but the Council itself was by the early 1970s beginning to lose its grip on the people's imagination as the major organ of development. Finally, as councillors voted for increases in their own monthly pay and allowances, and became the only ones to ride around in the reduced numbers of Council-owned vehicles, the people's mutterings about refusing to pay tax became more pronounced. The centre of governmental control now shifted to the North Hagen District headquarters at Muglamp, manned by public service personnel (kiaps). This complex, permanently staffed and in good contact with the township by both road and regular telephone service, has proved very effective in pulling administrative attention away from the area occupied by the Tipuka-Kawelka alliance and directing it to the interest of the Minembi-Kombukla pair (on this division see A. J. Strathern 1971b: 56–70).[2] There is no overt intention involved here on the part of government officers; it is a subtle effect of propinquity and convenience. What may have been intended was to allow the MP to consolidate his influence on the northern side and to balance this by administrative attention in the south; and it is to the problem of the MPs role that I turn next. Before I do so, however, it may be best to summarize the direction of the argument so far.

First, like all others in the Highlands, the Dei people experienced many effects from the initial introduction of shell valuables by Europeans. The source of valuables was not only outside their own clan areas, it was controlled by an alien set of people. An encompassing sense of hierarchy and dependency was thus set over the initial buoyancy of competition and prestige-seeking which followed pacification and the expansion of exchange networks. Second, the 'government' was seen at the apex of the new system of power, which was seen as both arbitrary and magical, founded on original possession of wealth and technology. Third, Local Government Councils, introduced to mediate between central government and the people, have had limited success in establishing an image as a source of 'government' in their own right; most recently people have even opposed the Council's collection of tax, charging that councillors use it for their own salaries and not to develop the area. Attention has switched back to the Government Office at Muglamp as a source of real decision-making; yet the contemporary kiaps, shorn of their power, are also a puzzle. Does the MP, then, complete the picture of government for the people?

The role of the MP

The position of Parua in Dei Council is remarkable. He has a dominating and determined character, preserving an air of challenge and assertiveness in every action he performs. He is fond of referring to himself by his father's name, Kuri, since the father was a noted big-man, who married ten wives and is seen as having united the Tipuka and Kawelka peoples in a profitable alliance following pacification patrols in 1945. Parua utilizes to the full his father's network of alliances and meticulously maintains the exchanges which support it, having long since dropped his earlier fulminations against *moka*, though he still calls people to greater efforts at business and money-making. He was in the Council from its inception as its Vice-President and later its President, and still gives the impression of being its most important decision-maker since he retained, with just a show of disinclination, his ordinary councillorship after being elected as MP. He has been seen riding into town with each kiap, executive officer, or clerk, of the Council, if not himself driving a Council vehicle, on matters of business which overlap Council affairs and his own. Since 1974 he has owned a grey Toyota Land Cruiser, presented to him *en masse* by the Kawelka at the last big *moka*. This was still running, somewhat haltingly and intermittently, in 1978.[3]

Parua owes his initial and second successful election largely to the Tipuka-Kawelka alliance, and to the absence of any serious rival within his half of the Council. He opposes the educated young men who may stand against him. For example, a trained kiap who belongs to Parua's own mother's clan in Kawelka, and a university graduate in Anthropology and Sociology, who, after completing course-work set up his own

Development Association in the Ganz River area, a hinterland within the Jimi on which Parua relies for votes (A. J. Strathern 1976b: 266). In the latter case Parua let it be known, when it looked as though the graduate might stand against him, that this potential rival had encouraged people not to pay Council tax and so should be prosecuted under the Local Government Council Act. He paid less attention to numerous murmurs of dissent concerning tax within his own alliance. But he has also consistently sought, as is perhaps expected by the Administration, and certainly by his followers, to 'pull in' benefits on a large scale for his part of the Council. After an abortive side-involvement in the 1968–71 Dei 'money cult' (A. J. Strathern 1979–80), he was set on mending his financial image as soon as he achieved status as an MP. He joined a development company which had been formed by a young mission-trained businessman, Goimba-Kot, from his own section of the Tipuka. After some belligerent episodes marked by accusations of profiteering, Parua has settled down to partnership, with Goimba as a director of this company. He is also a director of the Tigi Plantation Development Company, formed through the Council. He has gained support for part of the profits emerging from Tigi to be used to finance the purchase of a smaller plantation near the Wahgi, Nunga, to be run by people of a group with which the Tipuka have an ancient alliance. In 1975 and 1976, just before and after Independence, he was most active in attempting to set up a business development group based directly on his own alliance, in order to build a coffee-processing factory for the whole Council area, to be linked with a fleet of cars for buying coffee along the roads. It was an idea which had great attraction. Other development groups were beginning or were already in business (e.g. the Pipilika Association started by Michael Mel and Andrew Kei, and the Welyi-Kuta group, based on a consortium of Welyi, Kombukla, and Minembi groups).[4] Plantations were purchased as going concerns, but there was a perception that Europeans still controlled the larger corporate enterprises and held the keys to profit in relation to the outside world. The notion of building a factory for Dei itself was clearly designed both to unite the Council as an economic unit and to publicize Parua's own success as an influential MP prior to the 1977 elections. I was asked to provide a Voluntary Service Overseas (VSO) volunteer to help set up and run such a venture, and I duly held discussion and interviews with VSO personnel in Port Moresby and London. VSO were extremely helpful; an officer visited Parua's home, talked with leaders and wrote an assessment report. Yet the impetus failed, largely because of doubt among the people at large about the principle of such a venture. Once before, at the time of self-government, Parua had initiated a similar drive to collect money for a co-operative, and an initial set of contributions had been taken. But others, suspicious of entrusting money in this way, had counselled delay, and eventually these were withdrawn. So it was again. Parua was genuinely disappointed, and the northern side of Dei had indeed lost an opportunity. Parua was nevertheless re-elected in 1977, with a caucus of careful supporters acting as his electoral agents on the simple grounds that 'we elect by competition with the others', that is, if Kombukjla-Minembi put up candidates, as they did, this in itself was sufficient to unite Parua's own core supporters and in turn their allies behind him, in spite of some personal dissatisfactions.

Dissatisfaction really stems from perception of the MP's role in general. From the beginning, when Dei candidates first stood for national elections, in 1968 when Dei and Mul were one electorate, the most common statement made in speeches was that an MP must be a man strong enough to demand and obtain resources for his area, in presumed competition with other strong men. An MP who does not often speak in Parliament and who cannot point to tangible benefits he has brought home for his electors soon finds that his reputation is tarnished. The idea of participation at national level in policy-making for the whole country is less developed, although it may be more prominent, and more successfully stressed, in those electorates where the MP belongs to the ruling coalition, or better still, is a Minister. Parua belongs to the United Party, which, until late 1978 had no direct share in government, being confined to the role of opposition. By the same token, it has been much harder for him to claim any definite benefits brought to Dei. Although it is evident that he has surpassed his rivals both by his symbolic stature as an aggressive big-man and by his knowledge of government gained initially through Council work (A. J. Strathern 1976b: 284), it is less clear that he has been successful as a real patron or broker on behalf of his political clients within Dei. Indeed, his continuing identification with the Council and with corporate business done through it was harming his image by 1978. When it became known to some of the Kawelka that the Council's finance committee and subsequently the general body of councillors were proposing an expensive jaunt for a number of councillors to see the Philippines, and that Parua had proposed a motion of support for this, people's suspicions of an élite conspiracy between the MP and the Council in search of mutual profit began to harden. (In fact, the proposal was later abandoned, following adverse comment from government sources outside the Council.) There was similarly sour reaction to the news that MPs had recently voted for their own salaries to be raised. Neither piece of news was officially communicated to the people, perhaps because these events coincided with the Council's tax patrols. Instead, the information filtered through teachers in schools who were able to read newspaper reports.

A comparable level of mystery surrounds the activities of the MP and a handful of other councillors in their role as Directors of the Tigi plantation. Their meetings are held in Hagen township, not at Tigi itself. They receive a generous *per diem* allowance for attendance, and do not have to report back to the people at large on any decisions which are made. In all these ways, it was becoming apparent, to younger men among the Kawelka at least, that their MP was transforming himself into a different kind of big-man, one who did not depend on, or evince, direct reciprocity with themselves. His energetic support of an issue of social control which blew up in July 1978 between the Kawelka at Kuk and Tari settlers beside a neighbouring tea plantation (Tibi) did not entirely allay their feeling that politicians, like councillors, were by and large out for their own interests. It was apparent also that the Provincial Government would be created along the lines of the National Parliament and members elected to it in the same way. If so, they judged, the new members could be expected to develop their role along the same lines as existing MPs. Yet, overall, there was support for the new idea and some excitement at what it might bring.

My suggestions in this section have been first, that the MP has been elected largely on 'traditional' grounds, that is, that his status as a centre-man in an important alliance is reconfirmed through the Council system; second, that his association with the Council has enabled him to assume a wider political role, which may now be a drawback; and third that because he is perceived as a patron who must obtain resources from 'government', and because this expectation is not one he can readily fulfil, doubts about his role reflect forward to the idea of the Provincial Government.

The next section considers further aspects of the way in which matters of the kind already discussed feed into attitudes towards proposed Provincial Government.

Provincial Government

On Christmas Day 1977 the Kawelka Kundmbo clan, with which I live at Golke, held a meeting at which their Councillor, Ruin, reviewed issues which would be important in the coming year. The meeting was not well attended, in no way comparing with the massed occasions when pig are cooked for a funeral or given away live in *moka*. Two of the clan's four established major big-men attended, Roltinga and Mörl, Ndamba and Ai being absent and there was a good sprinkling of interested younger men in their thirties. Ruin, who is not outstandingly noted for his reports to the clan on Council affairs, nevertheless did a loyal job in warning people of the effects of the new Tribal Fighting Act which was about to come into force, urging that women should pay to travel on the clan truck, and that the men should start working bees in order to repair their road in the new year. The central part of his speech, loosely attached to these other issues, had to do with provincial government, as follows:

Last Friday I went out to the Council meeting. We had been called to attend by a man who will be involved in the work of the Provincial Government, in order to discuss how we shall find men to serve in it. Only fifteen – sorry sixteen – Councillors attended, others had disappeared in various directions to drink beer. So we were not able to make up our mind properly. He told us to return in January and to name many men we wanted. They have given five to Hagen Council, and five to Mid-Wahgi, since it had a big population similar to Hagen, and four each to Baiyer and Mul, and four to Dei, but we said Dei has a biggish population too and we would require five; and four to Mt Giluwe and to the Nebilyer area. After the candidates for election have been found, each one should pay K50 for his candidature. It does not matter whether they know Pidgin or not, for they will not go to a different place to talk, as MPs go to Parliament in Moresby. They will stay in our own area, divide out money, carry the people's problems on their shoulders, do those things. The boundaries of our Dei Council are wide [he enumerates them] and within it the Kendipi people are to find one man; at Glumant they are to find another; here in Tiki ward we have many people, and we shall find two [= four!] They will start work in the first month. Those who wish to stand for election should do so, then. The man who at a gathering of people divides pork out well, calls out the names of recipients well, who can climb trees and pollard them for a garden, who can swim across rivers – these are the kinds of men they want. The work will not be child's play; it will be a very strong type of work for tough men. So they will begin in January. And why are we going to get this thing, Provincial Government? It is because the central government sends money from its bank to a single bank for the Western Highlands in Hagen town, and that money is used for everything: road repairs, patrols, whatever. Well, the man who works with Provincial Government will divide that money, he will be like the man who makes the prayers over the pigs at a sacrifice, others just carry on work by their own inclinations, at random, but this man will be doing really important work. Those who stand for election will be in competition for the job, putting in their money as a 'bet'. Men such as our Oklembo Kuma [Vice-President of the Melpa Area Authority, who was expecting to get a ministry in the new government], and Waembe Wulyana, Kawelka Kont [previously a councillor], Kimbo Tep [Chief Magistrate of the Tigi Village Court] all those men who are strong, [*ombil penem*, all those men who have a bone] let them stand for election. It is just a matter of trying, a kind of game, and K50 is not much money, the sort of amount men spend on beer or cards in an evening. It will be like a race in which anyone who runs hard can win, and then the winner will be like the man with the knife who cuts up and divides the pig. It doesn't matter whether the candidates know how to read or write or not; I asked and was told it made no difference. I have spoken about cutting up a pig, that is my way of putting it, so you men who have the capability should stand for election; you understand my meaning. These men will look after the cement pipes we put in our roads as drains, they will look after the permanent-material houses, they will look after the town, the markets, road surfaces, plantations, coffee growing, every little thing, supplies of wire for cattle ranches, the upkeep of the airport – whatever you think of, these men will be in charge of it. That is why I say one of you men should stand. Kont is saying that he has already won, that there is no point in others standing [mutters and comments of 'Take no notice of him!']. It will not be like things are at present, when people say that the money for a project is down in Moresby and the papers have not been straightened out yet. Rather, we shall go right into the house where the money is and divide it out ourselves, sending it in different directions. We made self-government, and more recently Independence, now we shall make provincial government. And we should remember we are short of money,

we live in a poor place and we should not make so many *moka* with money; as it is we walk around and "pull" too much money off other people. Soon the time will come when a strong law will arrive and those people will take us to court and put us in gaol, so let us instead plant a great deal of coffee, do business, and get money, putting money *moka* second; let us follow the Lutheran and Catholic missions, build "house-lines" do good things, that is what I am telling you.'
(Speech by Councillor Ruin at Kawelka Kundmbo clan meeting, December 1977)

In this speech, the image of what government is about has not basically changed since the first election speeches of 1968. Government is about the division of money for projects. Where the money comes from is not examined, although the whole process is linked with the people gaining more money through business and adopting a new life-style. The difference between the original imagery and the present version is expressed succinctly: before, the money was divided up in Moresby, but now we shall have it here and divide it ourselves, just like a pig which we ourselves butcher. Nor would education matter: anyone with good sense and some local experience could stand. Small wonder that at least two young men of the clan, including Nikint, son of the major big-man Ndamba, said at once that they would stand against Kont, even though he was of their own tribe and they might therefore split the Kawelka vote.

As far as it went, Ruin's picture was quite accurate. Moreover, his imagery contained some warning hints of danger and hard work. He who divides pork is often accused of partiality or meanness; he who lops tree-branches or swims rivers is in physical danger. In other words, Ruin was urging that the new members would have to be men of scrupulous justice and also brave men who could stand up to difficulties and criticism. The resources would be there; all would depend on their division. His words may be related back to criticisms of the MP in the National Parliament: that he had turned to favouring councillors and the Council system as an élite network rather than caring for all the people, though his votes depended on them. One of the things Parua had rather conspicuously not attended to lately, his critics claimed, was his duty to visit the people and talk with them, handling their immediate local concerns and worries. He had not, that is, played his municipal role. Instead, he was always at meetings in town or in the capital, and who knew what he did there? (Indeed, it was true that the visited the town almost daily, and did not patrol widely in Dei on return from Parliament in September 1978.) Ruin, in saying that the new members would have to look after 'every little thing' (*mel nambel nambel*) was possibly also hinting that attention to local detail would be required, and that, since Parliament was so remote, the Provincial MPs would have, by contrast, to be very much on the spot.

One can infer, then, that while the new members' role was seen in the context of the same basic notion of 'government' as before, there was both a hope that they would benefit their local areas more directly than the national MP could, and that good standards of rectitude could be expected. With this proviso, people appeared keyed-up, and confident that Provincial Government was important, as something which might operate more effectively than either the Local Councils or the National Parliament in bringing real improvements to ordinary people.

I left Hagen on 2 January, 1978 and did not return until 18 July. By that time I found that interest in the new form of government had waned considerably, at least among the Kawelka people. The reason was simple. The Provincial Government had been delayed by several months, and no wide-scale elections had been held. Further, Kuma, who belongs to Parua's political alliance, did not become a minister in the provisional version of the government which was being set up, despite his previous status as Vice-President of the Area Authority. It rather appeared as though Mr John Maes, another Dei politician and businessman, would instead gain a position. John Maes is from the Kombukla-Minembi complex and is also important in the Welyi-Kuta axis of relations. His success would therefore mean the eclipse of the Tipuka-Kawelka hegemony, which, coupled with the shift of administrative power to Muglamp, would put further pressure on Parua to redress the balance within Dei. It was possibly not unconnected with this predicament that Parua at the time was himself interested in pursuing a different strategy.

In 1964, when the first national elections were held, Parua had supported Kaibelt-Diria, a Mid-Wahgi candidate, when Dei was included in the Minj electorate. Kaibelt had set the tone of patronage-oriented politics by claiming responsibility for the introduction of iron bridges to replace wooden logs and for the removal of the necessity for women to participate in road work. Parua had seen him as a new type of black man able to hold his own with Europeans. By now Kaibelt, who had left the United Party, become a minister, but, most recently, lost his attempt at re-election, was a figure from the past. Nevertheless Parua re-opened the issue of joining with Minj to form a separate Province, instead of one with Hagen and Mul. His actions clearly followed the Mid-Wahgi people's own battle through their Tuale Association, to claim a separate province for themselves away from Hagen, which has always been the centre for the Western Highlands. Parua's eastwards alliance with the Nelga people, who were involved in the takeover of Nunga plantation, and further plans to obtain the Kinjibi plantation not far from the Nangamp border, were clearly coincident with this idea of formally joining Mid-Wahgi. To do so would reinstate the northern half of Dei as central once more, and take from Muglamp its significance as the centre close to Hagen.

To date (December 1978) the issue of splitting the province into two is unresolved, although the initial Provincial Government and its ministries have been set up since mid-November, with a strong contingent of representation from the Mokei people, who have historically been important in setting up relations with the government in Hagen township. It did not look in September as though Dei would really join with the Wahgi or that the province would be split; but conflicts and tensions over 'dividing up the pig' are likely to remain.

Conclusions

In all political systems there are contradictory pictures of politicians. One view is that they are in office to serve the people; the opposite is that they are there to line their own pockets. In practice, of course, their strategies must be mixed; hence politics becomes a matter of compromises. Clearly, it will be the same with any provincial government. The Dei people have now become used to a whole series of experiments with new institutions: the Councils, the National Parliament, Village Courts, and now Provincial Government, each one presented as an answer to particular problems and as a part of some overall scheme for their development. They have become wary, and rightly so.

The overall situation is as I indicated in my three main points at the beginning of the paper. Local people are inevitably dependent for prosperity, at least in part, on the division or distribution of resources by institutional bodies outside their own area. They pay tax to councils, and these then distribute the money to projects. Central government sends money to pay for public servants and some rural development. Politicians and councillors are needed to make the case for their constituencies or wards, and then the people become also dependent on these individuals. It is true that they have power over them by electing or not electing them, yet such power is exercised only rarely and in between elections they have little say. It cannot be surprising, then, that politics is seen as a means of access to limited goods, limits defined by bodies such as central government, and that suspicion and doubt fix on the probity or skill of particular politicians. Provincial politicians will certainly face that same challenge of proving their worth to the people. Most importantly, they will not be able to transcend the straightforward application of the pig-butchering model unless they can, through provincial planning and through the genuine encouragement of local self-help, create a different idea of what development is about from that which has so far been generated. They will have to do so against the objective determination of relations which comes from dependence on cash-cropping and on subventions from the national government, itself supported by copper revenues and development loans. The most important matter to begin with, however, will be that which can be deduced from a part of Councillor Ruin's speech: that is, attention to local detail and concern in depth for local issues. It is in pursuit of that ideal that the Provincial Government is ostensibly being established, and if the new politicians can hold to it then this new tier of governmental structure may prove justified. If they cannot, not only will they be criticized for dividing the pig away from the people's direct scrutiny, but they will also be suspected of eating too much of it themselves.

Notes

1 This picture has been complicated, naturally, by the development of the National Parliament as the actual government, leaving the role of district officials anomalous.
2 It was also precisely the spot where an axe attack was made on Parua, when he attended the first opening of the police post (A. J. Strathern 1973, 1974). This was scarcely an auspicious way for the northern Dei people to be introduced to a new centre of law and order, and the event led to their avoidance of Muglamp for some years.
3 Parua used this vehicle mostly for family and clan purposes, in keeping with the fact that eventually he will have to call on his family and clan to raise cash for a return prestation.
4 The development of such groups has been facilitated by the Business Groups Act 1974.

References

Althusser, L. (1969) *For Marx*. London: Allen Lane.

Barth, F. (1966) *Models of Social Organization*. Occasional Publication no. 23. London: Royal Anthropological Institute.

—— (1975) *Ritual and knowledge among the Baktaman of New Guinea*. Oslo: Universitets Forlaget.

Bateson, G. (1936) *Naven*. Cambridge: Cambridge University Press.

Bloch, M. (1983) *Marxism and Anthropology*. Oxford: Clarendon Press.

Blong, R. J. (1982) *The Time of Darkness: Local Legends and Volcanic Reality in Papua New Guinea*. Canberra: Australian National University Press.

Belshaw, C. S. (1955) In Search of Wealth. American Anthropological Association Memoir 80 (57) 1, part 2.

Brandewie, E. (1981) *Contrast and Context in New Guinea Culture: the Case of the Mbowamb of the Central Highlands*. Studia Instituti Anthropos 39. St Augustin.

Brookfield, H. (1973) Full Circle in Chimbu: a Study of Trends and Cycles. In H. Brookfield (ed.) *The Pacific in Transition*. Canberra: Australian National University Press and London: Edward Arnold.

Brookfield, H. and White, J. P. (1968) Revolution or Evolution in the Prehistory of the New Guinea Highlands. *Ethnology* 7: 43–52.

Brown, P. (1963) From Anarchy to Satrapy. *American Anthropologist* 65: 1–15.

Brown, P. (1978) *Highlands Peoples of New Guinea*. Cambridge: Cambridge University Press.

Brown, R. (1973) *Rules and Laws in Sociology*. London: Routledge & Kegan Paul.

Bulmer, R. (1966) Birds as Possible Agents in the Propagation and Dispersal of the Sweet Potato. *Emu* 65: 165–82.

Burton, J. (in press) Quarrying in a Tribal Society. *World Archaeology*.

Callinicos, A. (1982) *Is There a Future for Marxism?* London: Macmillan.

Clark, J. (1982) Rusty Tractors and 'Skin Kristens': a Report on Socio-economic development in Pangia District, SHP. Field Report 5 to the University of Papua New Guinea.

De Lepervanche, M. (1967–68) Descent, Residence, and Leadership in the New Guinea Highlands. *Oceania* 38: 34–58, 163–89.

Didi, B. K. (1982) An Overview of the Traditional Religious Cults in the Lower Kaugel Valley of the Tambul Sub-District, WHP. *Oral History* IPNGS, Port Moresby.

Fitzpatrick, P. (1980) *Law and State in Papua New Guinea*. London: Academic Press.

Finney, B. R. (1973) *Big-men and Business: Entrepreneurship and Economic Growth in the New Guinea Highlands*. Canberra: Australian National University Press.

Force, R. W. and Bishop, P. (eds) (1981) *Persistence and Exchange: a Symposium*. Pacific Science Association, Honolulu.

Godelier, M. (1978) Infrastructures, Societies, and History. *Current Anthropology* 19 (4): 763–68.

Godelier, M. and Garanger, J. (1973) Outils de pierre, Outils d'acier. *L'Homme* 13 (3): 187–220.

Golson, J. (1981) Agriculture in New Guinea: the Long View. In D. Denoon and C. Snowden (eds) *A Time to Plant and a Time to Uproot: a History of Agriculture in Papua New Guinea*, IPNGS, Port Moresby.

—— (1982) The Ipomoean Revolution Revisited: Society and the Sweet Potato in the Upper Wahgi Valley. In A. J. Strathern (ed.) *Inequality in New Guinea Highlands Societies*. Cambridge: Cambridge University Press.

Gregory, C. A. (1982) *Gifts and Commodities*. London: Academic Press.

Harrison, S. J. (1982) Stealing People's Names. PhD thesis, Australian National University, Canberra.

Heaney, W. (n.d.) Report to the Western Highlands Provincial Government.

Hogbin, H. I. and Wedgwood, C. (1952–54) Local Grouping in Melanesia. *Oceania* 23, 24.

Hughes, I. M. (1978) Good Money and Bad: Inflation and Devaluation in the Colonial Process. In J. Specht and J. P. White (eds) *Trade and Exchange in Oceania and Australia*. Special issue, *Mankind* 11 (3): 308–18.

Kahn, J. S. and Llobera, J. R. (1981) *The Anthropology of Pre-capitalist Societies*. London: Macmillan.

Lingenfelter, S. (1978) Socio-economic Change in Oceania. *Oceania* 48 (2): 102–20.

Malinowski, B. (1948) *Magic, Science and Religion, and Other Essays*. Boston: Beacon Press.

Mawe, T. (1982) *Mendi Culture and Tradition: a Recent Survey*. National Museum, Port Moresby.

Meggitt, M. J. (1965) *The Lineage System of the Mae-Enga of New Guinea*. London: Oliver Boyd.

—— (1977) *Blood is their Argument. Warfare among the Mae-Enga Tribesmen of the New Guinea Highlands*. Palo Alto, Calif.: Mayfield.

Mennis, M. (1982) *Hagen Saga*. IPNGS Port Moresby.

Mitchell, W. E. (1978) *The Bamboo Fire*. New York: W. W. Norton.

Modjeska, N. (1982) Production and Inequality: Perspectives from Central New Guinea. In A. J. Strathern (ed.) *Inequality in New Guinea Highlands societies*. Cambridge: Cambridge University Press.

Morren, G. B. (1977) From Hunting to Herding: Pigs and the Control of Energy in Montane New Guinea. In T. P. Bayliss-Smith and R. G. Feachem (eds) *Subsistence and Survival*. London: Academic Press.

Radcliffe-Brown, A. R. (1952) *Structure and Function in Primitive Societies*. London: Routledge & Kegan Paul.

Rappaport, R. (1968) *Pigs for the Ancestors*. New Haven: Yale University Press.

Reay, M. (1959) *The Kuma: Freedom and Confirmity in the New Guinea Highlands*. Melbourne: Melbourne University Press.

Robbins, R. W. (1980) Missionaries in Contemporary Melanesia: Crossroads of Cultural Change. *Journal de la Société des Océanistes* 69: 261–78.

Rodman, O. and Cooper, O. (1979) *The Pacification of Melanesia*. Ann Arbor: University of Michigan Press.

Salisbury, R. F. (1962) *From Stone to Steel. Economic Consequences of a Technological Change in New Guinea*. Melbourne: Melbourne University Press for the Australian National University Press.

—— (1964) Despotism and Australian Administration in the New Guinea Highlands. *American Anthropology* 66.

—— (1970) *Vunamami*. Berkeley: University of California Press.

Scaglion, R. (ed.) (1981) *Homicide Compensation in Papua New Guinea: Problems and Prospects*. Port Moresby: Office of Information, for the Law Reform Commission.

Schwimmer, E. (1973) *Exchange in the Social Structure of the Orokaiva*. London: C. Hurst.

Sillitoe, P. (1979) Stone versus Steel. *Mankind* 12 (2): 151–61.

—— (1981) Pigs in Disputes. *Oceania* 51 (4): 256–65.

Strathern, A. J. (1970) Kiap, Councillor, and Big-Man. In C. Rowley (ed.) *Politics in Melanesia*. Port Moresby: University of Papua New Guinea and Australian National University.

—— (1971a) Wiru and Daribi Matrilateral Payments. *Journal of the Polynesian Society* 80: 449–62.

—— (1971b) *The Rope of Moka.* Cambridge: Cambridge University Press.

—— (1971c) Cargo and Inflation in Mount Hagen. *Oceania* 41: 255–65.

—— (1972) The Entrepreneurial Model of Social Change: From Norway to New Guinea. *Ethnology* 11: 368–79.

—— (1973) Political Development and Problems of Social Control in Mount Hagen. In R. J. May (ed.) *Priorities in Melanesian Development.* Port Moresby: University of Papua New Guinea.

—— (1974) When Dispute Procedures Fail. In A. L. Epstein (ed.) *Contention and Dispute.* Canberra: Australian National University Press.

—— (1976a) Transactional Continuity in Mount Hagen. In B. Kapferer (ed.) *Transaction and Meaning.* Philadelphia: Institute for the Study of Human Issues.

—— (1976b) Seven Good Men: the Dei Open Election. In D. Stone (ed.) *Prelude to Self-government.* Port Moresby: University of Papua New Guinea.

—— (1977a) Souvenirs de Folie chez les Wiru. *Journal de la Société des Océanistes* 56–7: 131–44.

—— (1977b) Contemporary Warfare in the New Guinea Highlands: Revival or Breakdown? *Yagl-Ambu* 4: 135–46.

—— (1978) Finance and Production Revisited: in Pursuit of a Comparison. In G. Dalton (ed.) *Research in Economic Anthropology* 1: 73–104.

—— (1979a) Gender, Ideology and Money in Mount Hagen. *Man* 14: 530–48.

—— (1979b) *Ongka: A Self Account by a New Guinea Big-Man.* London: Duckworth.

—— (1979–80) The Red-box Money Cult in Mount Hagen. *Oceania* 50: 88–102, 161–75.

—— (1982a) Social Change in Mount Hagen and Pangia. *Bikmaus* (IPNES) 3 (1): 90–100.

—— (1982b) Death as Exchange: Two Melanesian Cases. In S. Humphreys (ed.). *Mortality and Immortality.* London: Academic Press.

Strathern, M. (1968) *Popokl:* the Question of Morality. *Mankind* 6: 553–62.

—— (1972) Official and Unofficial Courts: Legal Assumptions and Expectations in a Highlands Community. *NGRU Bulletin* 47, Port Moresby.

—— (1978) The Achievement of Sex: Paradoxes in Hagen Gender-thinking. In E. Schwimmer (ed.) *The Yearbook of Symbolic Anthropology* 1: 171–202. London: C. Hurst.

—— (1982) Making a Difference: Connections and Disconnections in Highlands Kinship Systems. Paper delivered at Conference on Feminism and Kinship Theory, Rome.

Strauss, H. and Tischner, H. (1962) *Die Mi-Kultur der Hagenberg-Stämme.* Hamburg: Cram, de Gruyter.

Thompson, E. P. (1978) *The Poverty of Theory and Other Essays.* London: Merlin Press.

Townsend, W. H. (1969) Stone and Steel Tool Use in a New Guinea Society. *Ethnology* 2: 199–205.

Vicedom, G. F. and Tischner, H. (1943–48) *Die Mbowamb* (3 vols) Hamburg: Cram, de Gruyter.

Waddell, E. W. (1972) *The Mound Builders*, American Ethnological Society monograph 53. Seattle.

Wagner, R. (1967) *The Curse of Souw. Principles of Daribi Clan Definition and Alliance in New Guinea.* Chicago: University of Chicago Press.

—— (1974) *Habu.* Chicago: University of Chicago Press.

Watson, J. B. (1965) From Hunting to Horticulture in the New Guinea Highlands. *Ethnology* 4: 295–309.

—— (1967) Horticultural Traditions in the Eastern New Guinea Highlands. *Oceania* 38 (2): 81–98.

—— (1971) Tairora: the Politics of Despotism in a Small Society. In P. Lawrence and R. M. Berndt (eds) *Politics in New Guinea.* Nedlands: University of Western Australia Press.

Name index

Subject index